The Criminal Law Library—No. 2

MISUSE OF DRUGS

First supplement to second edition

PATRICK BUCKNELL, M.A. (Cantab.),

of the Inner Temple, Barrister

and

HAMID GHODSE, M.D., Ph.D., F.R.C.P., F.R.C.Psych., D.P.M.,

Professor and Director, Psychiatry of Addictive Behaviour, St. George's Medical School and Hospital, University of London; Consultant Psychiatrist, St. George's and Springfield University Hospitals, London

Law stated as at June 31, 1993

London   Sweet & Maxwell   1993

Published in 1993 by
Sweet & Maxwell Limited of
South Quay Plaza
183 Marsh Wall
London E14 9FT
Typeset by Mendip Communications Ltd.,
Frome, Somerset
Printed in Great Britain

A catalogue record for this book is available from the British Library.

ISBN Main work 0 08 040141 4
ISBN Supplement 0 421 48490 X

No natural forests were destroyed to make this product. Only farmed timber was used and replanted.

Contents

This supplement updates or amends chapters and appendices in the current edition of the main work. In addition, new chapters and appendices have been inserted. The list below sets out the chapters and appendices for which there is new material; new topics of particular importance not covered in the main work are in italic.

Table of Cases

Table of Statutes

Table of Statutory Instruments

xi

Table of Conventions

The Extent and Nature of Drug Problems: A Global Perspective

INTRODUCTION

2A.01 The use of mind-altering drugs of one sort or another has occurred throughout the history of mankind for both medical and religious purposes. Enhancement of physical well-being and heightened religious and mystical experiences were considered appropriate and legitimate reasons for the use of drugs; the relief of psychic pain, anxiety and emotional problems by means of drugs has always appeared to be more attainable than actually solving the underlying problems; drugs have also been used purely for hedonistic recreational intoxication. Man has probably always had some concern about the non-medical use of drugs, but the fact that there is far greater concern now is due to the greater understanding and awareness of the adverse health and social consequences which have followed the ever-increasing availability and use of drugs. These can now be found far from the communities where they were originally available and where they were used by the local population in a socially controlled and socially sanctioned manner.

Here one should emphasise the significance of the technological advances of the twentieth century: the ability to produce very pure and potent forms of these drugs; the availability of syringes and needles, and modern methods of transportation and communication. It is easy to understand how drug use, which has been going on for thousands of years without causing too many problems, has, in the twentieth century, become a global catastrophe. Undoubtedly, however, human greed for the acquisition of power and profit is an old motive for the production, distribution and marketing of drugs for non-medical use, without concern for the adverse consequences.

Practical planning for problems related to drug abuse requires knowledge of the number of people involved and the nature of their problems. Unfortunately, this information is not readily available: those involved may not perceive that they have a problem and, even if they

1

do, they may choose to conceal it, sometimes because their drug use is illegal.

Owing to the number of drugs that may be abused and the difficulties which ensue, no single epidemiological method is ever going to provide the "magic number" of those within a population with a problem related to drug abuse. Even if it did, the information would be useless because it would say nothing about the nature of the particular problems in context. Thus, when assessing drug abuse problems, one must be prepared to use a variety of methods, each of which contributes a "patch" or an area of information that may or may not blend or interconnect with the information from other enquiries, so that gradually a picture of drug abuse within the community, and the problems consequent upon this, emerges.

One way of finding out about patterns of drug use is to investigate the supply situation by obtaining information on production, importation, exportation and distribution. In practice, of course, reliable data can only be obtained about licit sources of supply as no official figures are kept on illicit practices. However, some information can be obtained about drug seizures and purchases made on the black market for investigation purposes. This data gives an idea of the availability, purity and costs of different drugs and further information can be obtained from sampling surveys of the general and drug-using populations, although this has problems of consistency and validity. Another way of investigating patterns of drug use is to assess the demand for and the actual consumption of particular (licit) drugs. Although such methods of inquiry are indirect methods, and the data obtained is unlikely to be absolutely accurate, its regular collection will show up changes in the supply of and demand for drugs and may, on occasion, give an indication of a developing abuse problem.

In this chapter and the following one, an attempt is made to give a picture of the extent and nature of the drug abuse problem in the United Kingdom and an outline of the problem in the rest of the world. The data presented is from a few official sources rather than from academic research institutes (Home Office Statistical Bulletins 1992, 1993; Department of Health Statistics, 1993; Thames Region Substance Misuse Database 1993; International Narcotics Control Board Report 1992; United Nations Drug Control Programme Report 1992.)

DRUG DEPENDENCE IN THE UNITED KINGDOM

2A.02   There are no reliable figures about drug dependence in the United Kingdom not least because it is very difficult to measure the extent of any activity which carries an associated stigma. Furthermore, fashions in many aspects of drug abuse can change rapidly and most of the information is retrospective in nature. Notwithstanding these caveats, there is no doubt that drug misuse increased dramatically during the 1980s and the Drug Advisory Council on the Misuse of Drugs in its 1988 Report, "AIDS and Drug Misuse, Part I" estimated that in 1986 there were in the United Kingdom between 75,000 and 150,000 misusers of notifiable drugs, such as heroin and cocaine and, in addition, a comparable number misusing a variety of non-notifiable drugs, such as amphetamines. These figures did not include cannabis misuse.

Home Office data from Addicts Index

2A.03   The statistics issued annually by the Home Office are based on the notification of addicts receiving one or more of the notifiable drugs, but as there are many addicts obtaining drugs illicitly and, therefore, intent on concealment from any authority, official statistics can only represent a proportion, and perhaps a changing proportion, of the total. Doctors are required to notify the Chief Medical Officer at the Home Office of patients whom they consider to be addicted to cocaine and a number of opioid drugs. However, many drug misusers have no need for medical treatment and may not come into contact with doctors. A (changing) proportion of misusers are not (yet) addicted to the drugs they misuse. Furthermore, as has already been stated, notification is not required for a large number of controlled drugs, such as amphetamines and barbiturates, which are misused and which can cause dependence.

It should be emphasised that the primary function of the Index is to reduce the possibility of a person receiving drugs from more than one doctor simultaneously, and it is successful in this respect. However, it is widely acknowledged that, for the reasons given above, the data available from the Index is of limited value, as those notified to the Home Office are probably only a small proportion of regular users. Nevertheless, although the data should be treated with some caution, it is generally considered useful for picking up trends and for illustrating general patterns within a restricted group of drug users.

Number of addicts (Fig. 1)

2A.04   It can be seen from the graph that the number of addicts notified to the Home Office increased from 14,785 at the end of 1989 to 24,703 by the end of 1992, an increase of 67 per cent. Within this, the number of new addicts notified in the last year rose by 21 per cent. to 9,663. This is the highest number of new addicts ever recorded in one year and, at the same time, the number of re-notified addicts increased by 17 per cent. to

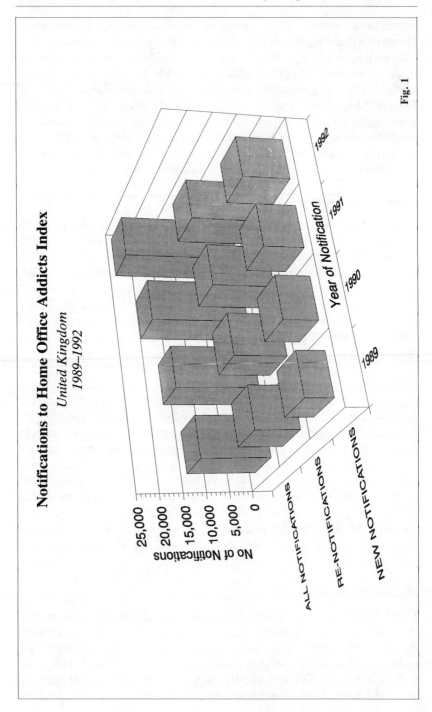

Notifications to Home Office Addicts Index

*United Kingdom
1989–1992*

Fig. 1

15,040. It has been suggested that some of this increase may have been the result of efforts by agencies to attract more addicts into treatment because of fear of AIDS. There might also be greater awareness of notification procedures and obligations by the doctors as a result of the establishment of the Regional Substance Misuse Databases by Health Authorities. Although the extent and nature of drug misuse varies considerably from one area to another, the most extensive drug abuse problems in the United Kingdom occur in some of the major cities.

Age and sex

2A.05 Both the age and sex of new addicts remained relatively stable during the 1980s. However, the number in the under-21 years age group, which fell in 1989, rose again by 38 per cent. in 1992. Seventy-four per cent. of the new addicts in 1992 were under the age of 30 and 18 per cent. were under 21. Although the average age of all addicts (not just new addicts) has risen steadily since the mid-1980s, the average age for new addicts in 1992 fell for the first time since 1985 to just under 27. The proportion of females has been steady throughout the last decade and just under one-quarter of new addicts in 1992 were female, a lower proportion than for the last 15 years. In summary, therefore, most addicts are men aged between 21 and 34.

Drugs of addiction (Fig. 2)

2A.06 The common drugs to which addiction is reported are heroin, methadone, dipipanone, cocaine and morphine in order of frequency. One-fifth of notified addicts were reported to be polydrug addicts.

Heroin was the most common drug of addiction for new addicts notified throughout the 1980s, with the proportion increasing from 72 per cent. in 1980 to 93 per cent. in 1985 and then declining steadily to 79 per cent. in 1992. This, perhaps, reflected the availability of heroin during that period. In 1992, 7,658 new heroin addicts were notified, an increase of 1,330 on the number in 1991.

The number of new methadone addicts increased by a staggering 48 per cent. in 1991 and by 14 per cent. in 1992 to 2,493. This increase is probably a reflection of more new addicts being treated with methadone, particularly when the drug of addiction for which treatment is sought is not one of the 14 notifiable drugs.

The number of those reported as addicted to dipipanone fell slightly in 1992 and the total is substantially less than in the early 1980s. This is an indication of the reduced availability of this drug following control being placed on its prescription in 1984.

The number of new cocaine addicts increased in 1992 to 1,131.

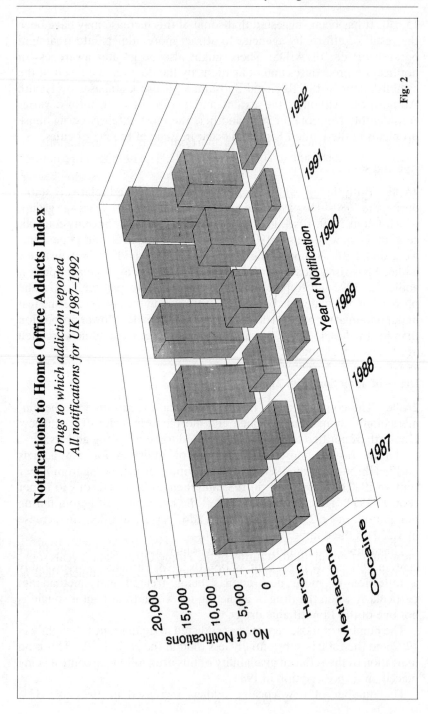

Fig. 2

Although this is a small proportion (12 per cent.) of new notifications, it is a higher percentage than in previous years. Despite large seizures of cocaine, its misuse has so far not created a significant demand for medical treatment.

Heroin and methadone remained the most common drugs of addiction among re-notified addicts in 1992, with some 9,300 addicted to heroin and 7,500 addicted to methadone, 29 per cent. more than in 1991. As with new addicts, the increase in the proportion addicted to methadone has been substantial, rising to 50 per cent in 1992. The number of re-notified addicts reported as addicted to cocaine rose by 28 per cent. to 820, accounting for only 5 per cent. of re-notified addicts.

Notifiable drugs were prescribed to 5,742 new addicts and 11,803 re-notified addicts at their first notification in 1992. In total, 70 per cent. of those treated were prescribed methadone alone or with other drugs. Addicts notified by general practitioners were less likely to be prescribed notifiable drugs than those notified by hospital treatment centres.

General practitioners accounted for 36 per cent. of first notifications of both new and re-notified addicts in 1992, while hospitals and treatment centres notified over 50 per cent.; prison medical officers notified 10 per cent. and police surgeons about 4 per cent.

Death among notified addicts

2A.07   By definition, mortality statistics focus on the most serious forms of drug abuse, those from which the person has died. Causes of death are numerous; they include overdose (suicidal, accidental or homicidal), side-effects of drugs, complications of non-sterile self-injection, and functional impairment that increases the risk of serious accident. In the United Kingdom very few scientific studies on the mortality of addicts have been carried out. However, the Home Office keeps a list of those addicts removed from the current Index by reason of death. Obviously, the information refers only to addicts known to the Home Office in the first place and, as we have seen, this is by no means complete. Bearing these limitations in mind, scrutiny of the Home Office data reveals some interesting facts. For example, 340 previously notified addicts died in 1991, which continues the upward trend of recent years. Of all addicts who died between 1986 and 1991, about 17 per cent. were originally notified less than 12 months before death, 34 per cent. within two years of death and three-fifths within five years. The main cause of drug addicts' deaths remained overdose and, where the drugs used were recorded, opiates and apoids were involved in about three-quarters of cases. The mortality pattern of the addicts first notified in each year from 1986 to 1990, shows that 0.7 per cent. of addicts died within 12 months of first being notified, 0.5 per cent. within the second year, and another 0.5 per cent. in the third year. This compares with figures from Ghodse *et al.* "Deaths of Drug Addicts in the United Kingdom 1967-1981" (1985) 290 B.M.J. 425 covering the much longer period 1967–1979, which showed 3 per cent. dying in the first year, 1.9 per cent. in the second year and 0.7 per cent. in the third year. The cause of the apparent decrease in death rate in recent years is difficult to establish from the statistics alone, but may be due to the changes in availability of certain drugs, such as barbiturates, the provision of more and better treatment services and to more effective education of the public.

2A.08   The national statistics of drug-related death, provided by the Office of Population Censuses and Surveys (OPCS) for England and Wales, and by the General Register Offices of Scotland and Northern Ireland for the rest of the United Kingdom, are another source of mortality data. These offices classify causes of death using the Ninth Revision of the International Classification of Diseases (ICD 9). In 1991, there were nearly 1,360 deaths in the United Kingdom where drug dependence or abuse of controlled drugs was somehow implicated as a cause. Over 300 deaths were specifically attributed to drug dependence/ abuse while the remaining deaths resulted from accidental poisoning or suicide. The total number of deaths in which drug dependence/abuse was considered to be an underlying cause more than quadrupled between 1981 and 1991. The use of volatile substances which are not controlled drugs accounted for 40 per cent. of the increase.

Home Office data on seizures and offenders dealt with (Figs. 3 & 4)

2A.09   The data presented in the Home Office report on seizures and offenders relates to all controlled drugs and therefore offers information on a much wider range of illicit drug-taking behaviour. However, since it only covers seizures of drugs and persons dealt with for offences involving controlled drugs, the picture it provides is still fairly limited.

While changes in drug seizure and offenders do not necessarily imply changes in the prevalence of the misuse of controlled drugs, they may reflect changed demand for these substances. It is acknowledged, however, that other factors such as changes in the direction and effectiveness of enforcement effort, and changes in recording and reporting procedures may be significant.

2A.10   In 1991, seizures of drugs increased by 15 per cent., a similar increase to that reported in 1990, but less than in the two previous years. As in earlier years, the vast majority of seizures in 1991 were of cannabis and other Class B drugs which rose by 15 per cent. to 63,700. Seizures of Class A rose by 20 per cent. to 8,500, largely due to a greater number of

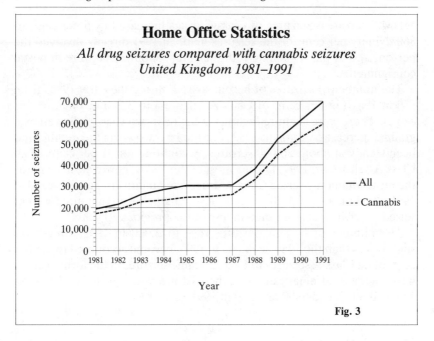

Home Office Statistics

All drug seizures compared with cannabis seizures
United Kingdom 1981–1991

Fig. 3

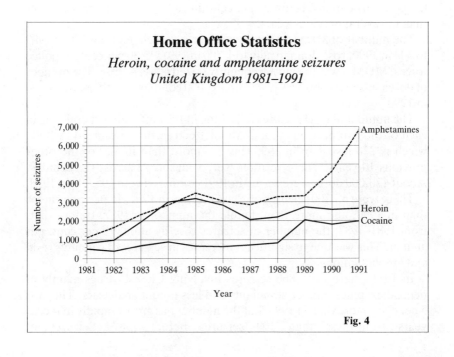

Home Office Statistics

Heroin, cocaine and amphetamine seizures
United Kingdom 1981–1991

Fig. 4

MDMA seizures. Seizures of Class C drugs increased by 5 per cent. to 860. Ninety per cent. of the seizures made in 1991 directly involved the person, and of the remaining 7,100 seizures, about 3,900 were in postal consignments.

The number of seizures of heroin soared during the early 1980s from 820 in 1981 (35 per cent. of Class A seizures) to 3,200 in 1985 (65 per cent.). There were slight reductions in the next two years, followed by a gradual increase to 2,700 in 1989. For the last two years the number has been steady at about 26,000 seizures, accounting for 31 per cent. of all Class A seizures in 1991. During most of the 1980s, however, heroin was the most commonly seized Class A drug. The quantity of heroin seized in 1991 (490 kg), although 20 per cent. less than the record amount (600 kg) seized in 1990, was more than in any of the previous 10 years.

The number of cocaine seizures rose to 2,000 in 1991, which was slightly less than the 1989 peak. As in 1990, cocaine accounted for 25 per cent. of all Class A seizures in 1991. Cocaine seizures in the form of crack have increased dramatically over the past few years, from 30 in 1989 to 140 in 1989, 320 in 1990 and 580 in 1991.

2A.11   A record quantity (nearly 1.1 tonnes) of cocaine was seized in 1991, 470 kg more than in 1990. The average purity of cocaine seized by the police rose to just below 50 per cent. in 1991, although this was lower than in several previous years.

The number of MDMA (Ecstasy) seizures, which fell from 770 in 1989 to 400 in 1990, rose dramatically to 1,700 in 1991. In 30 per cent. of police forces, MDMA was the most frequently seized Class A drug. The number of doses seized in 1991 was just over 365,000 compared with about 44,000 in 1990.

The number of LSD seizures fell a little in 1991 after almost doubling in each of the two previous years. About 1,600 seizures occurred in 1991, which is 220 less than in 1990, but far more than in any of the other previous 10 years. These seizures were widespread across the country. About 170,000 doses were seized in 1991 compared with 295,000 in 1990.

There were 63,700 seizures of Class B drugs in 1991, 15 per cent. more than in 1990, and more than double the number in 1987. Before that, from 1981–1987, the number of seizures rose by about 10 per cent. per annum. This was due to significant increases in seizures of cannabis resin and amphetamines.

In 1991, there were 860 seizures involving Class C drugs mainly of benzodiazepines, milder stimulants and less potent analgesics. This was 5 per cent. more than in 1990, but the number has grown rapidly in recent years from less than 100 seizures before 1987. Seizures of benzodiazepines (480) and of buprenorphine (340), alone or in combination with other drugs, were the main Class C drugs reported.

Persons dealt with for drug offences

2A.12 The number of persons dealt with for drug offences has continued to rise, and the total number reported to the Home Office in 1991 was 54,000, 5 per cent. more than in 1990. Due to the increased use of cautioning, there was a particularly large rise in the number of persons not dealt with at court, which increased by 20 per cent. from 20,500 in 1990 to 24,500 in 1991, while the number of cases dealt with at court fell by 1 per cent. to 29,500. This was the first fall since 1986, when the reduction was related to the general drop in indictable proceedings associated with changes in criminal justice procedures. The total number of persons found guilty, cautioned or dealt with by compounding grew steadily from 17,900 in 1981 to 27,000 in 1985. There was a fall in 1986 to 23,900 and then a steady increase to 47,000 in 1991. Overall, in the United Kingdom, about 55 per cent. of drug offenders were sentenced at court, while the remainder were cautioned or dealt with by compounding. The proportion of persons cautioned was 1 per cent. and 2 per cent. in 1981 and 1982, but has increased substantially in each of the last nine years to reach almost 45 per cent. in 1991. This is because of the growing practice among most police forces in England and Wales of cautioning first time offenders found in possession of small amounts of cannabis and some other drugs for personal use.

Although the number of male drug offenders rose by 5 per cent. between 1990 and 1991, the number of female offenders fell by 2 per cent., and accounted for under 10 per cent. of the total. The proportion of female offenders has ranged between 10 per cent. and 15 per cent. over the last 10 years. Forty per cent. of offenders were aged under 21, but this age group accounted for 85 per cent. of the total increase in offenders. The average age of offenders declined to 24 years, continuing the steady fall observed since 1987, when the average age was nearly 26. In comparison with the total population in the 17–29 age group, the proportion of offenders has more than doubled since 1986. In 1991 there were 4.7 drug offenders per 1,000 population aged 17–20, compared to 1.5 in 1986, 3.35 per 1,000 population aged 21–24 (1.5 in 1986), just under 2 per 1,000 population aged 25–29 (just over 1 in 1986), about 0.6 per 1,000 population aged under 17 (0.1 in 1986) and around 0.25 per 1,000 population of 30 years and over (little change since 1986).

Type of offence

2A.13 Unlawful possession of drugs remained the most common offence in 1991, as it was in previous years. Throughout the last decade, the majority of offenders were found in possession of cannabis. The number of "trafficking" offenders fell to 6,300 in 1991, 350 fewer than in 1990. This was mainly due to the falling number of unlawful import or export offenders. "Trafficking" offenders have also declined as a proportion of all offenders over the last three years from around 20 per cent. in 1987 to 15 per cent. in 1990 and 1991.

In 1991, for the second year running, more people were cautioned than fined, although this was once the most usual method of dealing with drug offenders. Thus, the proportion fined, which was 65 per cent. in 1981 fell to around 40 per cent. between 1987 and to 35 per cent. in 1990, and to 30 per cent. in 1991. This corresponds to the increased use of cautioning which has risen from 1 per cent. in 1981 to nearly 45 per cent. in 1991. The number of sentences of immediate custody also fell in 1991 to 3,300: the smallest number since 1983. However, the type of action taken varies considerably according to the age of the offender and the type of offence.

SUMMARY

2A.14 It is quite apparent that a wide range of drugs is available and used in most regions in the United Kingdom with cities having a greater share of these problems. Polydrug use and concurrent alcohol use is common as is the use and misuse of psychotropic medications. Reports from various drug agencies and treatment centres confirm official figures, including those of the Home Office, and it is clear that drugs of all types are widely available, and that the number of people using them and having associated medical, social and legal problems has increased. However, certain features of the data indicate a relatively steady state in some aspects of drug abuse and dependence problems. What is happening in the United Kingdom can be better understood and appreciated in the context of what is happening in Europe and the rest of the world.

The International Drug Problem

INTRODUCTION

2B.01 The problem of drug abuse that has preoccupied the United Kingdom during the last quarter-century has not been confined to this country. There is worldwide concern about all aspects of drug abuse, although specific drug problems may be of greater importance in some areas than in others. Despite a great deal of international interest and efforts by many countries at local, national and regional levels, the situation worldwide remains grim. Illicit production, trafficking and abuse of drugs, together with attendant violence and corruption, continues to impair public health in virtually all countries and has created a great deal of human suffering, loss of productivity and various social and economic problems with the threat of politic instability. Well-organised and well-financed international criminal trafficking organisations continue to produce and smuggle large quantities of opiates and cocaine throughout the world and there is alarming evidence of criminals and traffickers in South-East Asia and South America engaging in joint ventures, smuggling drugs to profitable markets. Cocaine, for example, which was once abused mainly in America and Europe, now threatens the Middle East, Africa, South-East Asia and Australia.

Without doubt, drug problems are closely linked to social, economic and political problems, and progress in all of these areas would contribute to the alleviation of drug abuse problems. The effect of recent changes in military, economic and political situations throughout the world on drug abuse problems has yet to be demonstrated, but it seems clear that greater instability in the world provides more opportunity for international traffickers and criminal organisations to exploit the situation, with consequent loss of human life and increased suffering.

The problem is further complicated by the emergence of lobbies to legalise the non-medical use of drugs and to permit their recreational use. This approach, which may be perceived as an indication of despair in the fight against drug abuse, is not currently permissible under the existing Conventions. While in theory these Conventions could be amended to permit the recreational use of drugs under international control, the arguments in favour of legalisation are generally considered to be simplistic, disregarding the consequent increase in public health problems.

INTERNATIONAL RESPONSES

2B.02   International collaboration is the cornerstone of the fight against the activities of drug traffickers and this has been recognised by the United Nations agencies which have increased their efforts and drug programmes in various countries around the world. This need, for international measures to control drug abuse and dependence has been recognised for a long time and a number of multilateral treaties have been signed over the years. Most important are the three Conventions (Single Convention on Narcotic Drugs 1961, as amended by the 1972 Protocol; Convention on Psychotropic Substances 1971; Convention Against Illicit Traffic in Narcotic Drugs and Psychotropic Substances 1988) designed to ensure the safe use of potentially dangerous psychoactive substances and to prevent their abuse; they also deal with drug trafficking and related issues.

By 1992, there were 135 parties to the Single Convention on Narcotic Drugs of 1961, of which 110 were parties to the Convention in its amended form (Convention as amended by the 1972 Protocol). The number of parties to the Convention on Psychotropic Substances of 1971 stood at 109. The Convention Against Illicit Traffic in Narcotic Drugs and Psychotropic Substances of 1988 came into force on November 11, 1990, and, as at November, 1992, 67 States and the European Economic Community Member States had become parties to this Convention.

2B.03   An important component of the international response to drug abuse is the International Narcotics Control Board, which has been given specific responsibilities by the Conventions:

> "The Board shall endeavour to limit the cultivation, production, manufacture and use of drugs to an adequate amount required for medical and scientific purposes and to ensure their availability for such purposes.
> The Board shall also endeavour to prevent illicit cultivation, production and manufacture of, and illicit traffic in and use of drugs."

In carrying out its responsibility, the Board is enjoined to act in collaboration with governments and to maintain continuing dialogue with them to further the aims of the Conventions. These require the Board to prepare an annual report on its work, analysing the control situation worldwide.

In this context, the Board examines and reports on substance misuse in various regions of the world. Opiates, of course, remain, as they have been for centuries, very significant substances for misuse. However, establishing the extent of this and, in particular, establishing the extent of illicit cultivation and trafficking, is complicated by the fact that there is legal cultivation and trade to meet legitimate need for opiates for medical and scientific purposes.

DEMAND FOR OPIATES FOR MEDICAL AND SCIENTIFIC PURPOSES

2B.04   Over the past 20 years, the worldwide consumption of opiates has been fairly steady, at about 200 tonnes of morphine equivalent annually, with codeine accounting for about 160 tonnes of this. Consumption of dihydrocodeine and morphine has been increasing and reached 18 tonnes and 11 tonnes of morphine equivalent respectively in 1991. It should be noted that the consumption of morphine is related mainly to its use as an analgesic in the treatment of cancer patients. However, the consumption of other opiates has either declined or remained unchanged. Due to climatic conditions and economic, social and policy considerations, the global production of opiate raw material fluctuates from year to year. During the first part of the 1980s, it averaged 207 tonnes in morphine equivalent annually, but in the latter part of the 1980s it fell to a level below consumption. However, the production of opiate raw material exceeded consumption by about 40 tonnes in 1991 and 50 tonnes in 1992.

The diversion of narcotic drugs from licit trade at global level has been relatively rare, and whenever this occurs, the quantities involved very small indeed compared with the volume of illicit transactions. This is also true for narcotic drugs in the domestic wholesale market, indicating that national and international control measures are largely effective for this group of substances.

DIVERSION OF PSYCHOTROPIC SUBSTANCES

2B.05   The control of the diversion of psychotropic substances from licit manufacture and trade into the illicit market has been less successful. However, control of substances included in Schedule 2 of the 1971 Convention, under which international trade is controlled by a mandatory system of import and export authorisation and for which a simplified estimate system has been operating successfully during the

1980s, has proved to be successful too. The worldwide reduction of stocks of methaqualone in line with declining medical requirements is a good example of the effectiveness of control measures for substances in Schedule 2 and there has been a similar decline in fenethylline stocks since its inclusion in Schedule 2 in 1986. However, there have been large diversions of substances included in Schedules 3 and 4 of the 1971 Convention, proving that this control mechanism for international trade is ineffective. For example, the inclusion of pemoline in Schedule 4 has had little impact on its illicit traffic and since 1989, when pemoline was subjected to international control, the equivalent of 1,500 million tablets exported from manufacturing countries in Europe were said to have been destined for illicit use.

THE GLOBAL DRUG PROBLEM SITUATION

2B.06   To put the United Kingdom's drug problem into an international perspective, a thumbnail sketch is provided of the situation in other regions, based on the report of the International Narcotics Control Board.

Africa

2B.07   Cannabis is the most abused drug in Africa and is grown throughout the continent. Large scale cultivation occurs in Morocco, both to satisfy domestic illicit demand and to produce cannabis resin, which is smuggled into Europe. While Morocco is one of the world's biggest sources of cannabis resin, Egypt also receives supplies of this drug from Lebanon.

The abuse of stimulants constitutes a major problem in many parts of Africa with the drugs being smuggled in from Europe. In particular, illicit traffic in pemoline has reached enormous dimensions, especially in Nigeria. Large amounts of other psychotropic substances are also diverted from licit sources as well as being manufactured in clandestine laboratories.

In the Horn of Africa, khat (*Catha edulis*) poses a different problem. It is cultivated mainly in Ethiopia, Kenya and Yemen and, although most is consumed locally or in neighbouring countries, freeze-dried or vacuum-packed leaves are now being shipped to Europe. As khat is not subject to international law, some countries have introduced national control measures to prevent its importation.

Although opiate abuse is comparatively rare in Africa, a few cases of intravenous heroin abuse have been reported. In the light of the popularity of stimulants in this region, another worrying development is the reported increase in cocaine abuse. This may be due in part to countries in West and North Africa increasingly being used as transit states for cocaine from South America destined for Europe.

Asia

2B.08 The East and South-East Asia region continues to be a major source of illicit heroin, with opium being processed into heroin in clandestine laboratories in the border areas of the Laos People's Democratic Republic, Mayanmar and Thailand. Increasingly China is used as a transit country for illicit heroin bound for Hong Kong and Macau, although Bangkok is a principal centre for heroin traffic by sea, air and overland via the Malaysian peninsula.

In addition to heroin, cannabis remains one of the most abused and trafficked substances in the region with the Laos People's Democratic Republic, the Phillipines and Thailand being the principal producer countries. In Japan, however, and in the Phillipines and Thailand, there is increasing concern about the abuse of, and illicit traffic in, stimulants, mainly methamphetamine, with the major source being the Taiwan Province of China. Due to the similarities of amphetamine and cocaine, and because of a sudden increase in cocaine seizures in Japan, the authorities there fear an increase in cocaine abuse may be imminent.

Elsewhere in Asia, Bangladesh is increasingly being used as a transit country for illicit drugs and in North India, where intravenous heroin abuse has been spreading, there has been a sharp increase in the number of individuals with HIV infection. Also in India, despite a ban on the manufacture of methaqualone, there has been a drastic increase in seizures of the drug, mostly bound for Africa.

Oceania

2B.09 Cannabis remains the most readily available drug of abuse in Australia, and although some of the cannabis found on the illicit market has been smuggled into the country, some is cultivated locally. Cocaine and heroin also continue to be available in most states in Australia, and amphetamine abuse is widespread. Amphetamines are manufactured in local clandestine laboratories, mainly in Victoria, but some have been smuggled in from other countries, particularly the Phillipines. LSD and MDMA are abused by young people, usually in conjunction with other drugs and alcohol.

Near and Middle East

2B.10   The abuse of heroin and opium remains the main problem in the Near and Middle East, although cannabis is commonly used in many countries. They are also seriously affected by large scale illicit traffic in psychotropic substances, mainly stimulants.

A particular problem is posed by heroin addiction among Afghan refugees, which has reached alarming proportions. Because of the constantly changing political and security situation, an accurate estimate of illicit opium production has not been possible. However, it has been estimated that this may exceed 1,000 tonnes annually. Illicit heroin manufacture has also increased in Afghanistan and large amounts of both opium and heroin leave the country bound for the West, through Iran and Pakistan. In Pakistan itself, illicit poppy cultivation is mainly in the North West Frontier Province, where substantial amounts of morphine and heroin are manufactured locally. It was estimated in 1988 that there were more than 300,000 opiate-dependent individuals in Pakistan and between 1983 and 1990, an average of 25 tonnes of opium, originating primarily in Afghanistan and Pakistan, were seized annually in the Islamic Republic of Iran.

Original, counterfeit and fake fenethylline tablets are smuggled from European countries, mainly Bulgaria and the former Yugoslavian states, to some countries in the region. During the 1980s, nearly 30 million tablets were seized, most destined for Saudi Arabia, and in 1991, nearly 4 million tablets were seized in Jordan, Saudi Arabia, Syria, Turkey and the United Arab Emirates.

Europe

2B.11   Although most attention is focused on the illicit use of heroin and cocaine, cannabis is still the most popular drug of abuse in Europe as a whole. The amount of cannabis seized has remained fairly stable, but the amount of cannabis resin appears to be increasing. Principally, this originates in Morocco although occasional consignments also arrive from Lebanon or South-West Asian countries.

More locally, cannabis is grown in the Netherlands for a variety of legal purposes, but the rapid spread of its illicit cultivation is a cause for concern, heightened by the fact that its THC content is much higher than in varieties from abroad. This leads to fears that the Netherlands could become a significant regional supplier of cannabis. Within the Netherlands itself, the government has a policy of tolerating cannabis abuse and sales of up to 30 grammes of cannabis products in so-called coffee shops, of which there are between 1,000 and 2,000. However, there is evidence that some are being used by traffickers and that other drugs are also sold there. A number of shops have consequently been closed. Overall, it is estimated that there are between 550,000 and 600,000 regular cannabis abusers in the Netherlands.

The situation *vis-à-vis* heroin abuse varies from country to country, although several are now reporting an upward trend with a substantial increase in the number of deaths due to heroin overdose. The heroin sold on the illicit market in Europe, mainly originates from the "Golden Triangle" in South-East Asia and the "Golden Crescent" (Afghanistan and Pakistan). It is estimated that 70–80 per cent. used to reach Europe via the Balkan route, travelling through the Islamic Republic of Iran and then through Turkey, Bulgaria and former Yugoslavia before reaching Austria.

2B.12 The disruption caused by the war in Yugoslavia has diverted this conventional route and the transit road through Bulgaria, Rumania, Hungary and Czechoslovakia is now popular. The Caucasian Republics, Greece and Cyprus are also acknowledged to be important transit countries. The amount and frequency of cocaine seizures are also increasing. It is mainly transported from South American countries to southern Europe, where some clandestine processing laboratories have been discovered; however, some arrives via countries in West and North Africa, and African heroin couriers often carry cocaine too.

The abuse of amphetamines, including the hallucinogenic MDMA (Ecstasy) is widespread in Europe and particularly in Nordic countries, where amphetamine is the main drug of abuse. The Netherlands and Poland are the principal suppliers, and the former is also a significant source of LSD, the use of which appears to be re-emerging in some countries.

Although there are a few reports on the abuse of hypnotics, sedatives or anxiolytics, dependence on them is common in many European countries. The prevalence of dependence and related public health and social problems are often underestimated, and these are made worse because of the frequency of polydrug abuse, usually associated with alcohol abuse.

2B.13 Two factors warrant particular consideration in any discussion on trends in drug abuse in Europe. The first is the Single European Act, (which was signed at Luxembourg and The Hague on February 17 and 28, 1986) permitting the free movement of persons, goods, services and capital within the European Community. This may have a significant impact on drug abuse problems.

The dramatic changes in the countries of Eastern Europe and in the new Commonwealth of Independent States (CIS) member states may be expected to be equally important. In particular, most CIS member states have inadequate drug legislation and drug control administration; there are often no controls at the new internal borders so that drugs can be easily transported across them. Furthermore, these countries lack structures for the treatment, rehabilitation and social care of drug-dependent persons, and lack professional experience in these fields.

A particularly serious situation exists in Poland, where current regulations are inadequate to deal with the various international criminal organisations that have recently increased their activities there.

Americas

2B.14   In the countries of North America, the drug problem remains a major item on the public health and social policy agenda. In Canada, cannabis products remain the most widely available and abused drugs although there are some indications of an overall reduction in their abuse. This is also apparent in the United States of America where the abuse of cannabis has been declining steadily since 1979, when there were approximately 22 million abusers compared with 9.7 million in 1991. The number of emergencies related to cannabis abuse has also declined by 31 per cent. However, there has been a marked increased in the potency of the cannabis on the illicit market mainly because of the high THC content of cannabis plant varieties cultivated indoors; the average THC content of the unpollinated and seedless (sinsemilla) cannabis was 11.7 per cent. compared with an average THC content of "commercial grade" cannabis of 3.1 per cent.

The abuse of heroin in the United States has remained at approximately the same level for the past four years, and it appears that heroin abuse has decreased significantly among young, occasional abusers. Some heroin (and cannabis) is smuggled into the U.S.A. across the Mexican border and the purity of heroin available at retail level has increased significantly to 36 per cent. compared with less than 10 per cent. during the 1970s and early 1980s. The report in the summer of 1992 of 30 fentanyl-related deaths may indicate the emergence of a new type of opiate abuse in the U.S.A.

Cocaine abuse, which showed a significant downward trend in the U.S.A. in the mid-1980s rose again in 1991, when it was estimated that there were about 1.9 million cocaine abusers. Cocaine abuse remains high in Canada too, with seizures totalling more than 1.2 tonnes in 1991.

South and Central America and the Caribbean

2B.15   Most countries in South and Central America and the Caribbean are being used more and more frequently to convey or to store illicit drugs. In particular, they play a major role in the trans-shipment of cocaine to Europe and to North America and of chemicals to countries where illicit cocaine manufacture takes place. The abuse of cocaine is increasing in all of these countries, the smoking of coca paste mixed with tobacco or cannabis ("basuco") being the most frequent form of drug abuse among youth in Bolivia, Colombia and Peru. Although coca-leaf chewing appears to be decreasing in Bolivia, the abuse of coca products is increasing and is a particular cause for concern among street children. Illicit poppy cultivation is also creating new problems, while cannabis is being grown illicitly and abused.

SUMMARY

2B.16   For drug abuse the global picture is gloomy, and it appears that most common drugs which are controlled by the international Conventions are abused in most parts of the world. Although there are some differences in the prevalence of this abuse, the similarities between different parts of the world are more striking than the differences: the abuse of heroin by injection is becoming more widespread; cocaine abuse is becoming more international in the true sense of the word and cannabis appears to be everywhere.

The issues of psychotropic drug production, of their distribution, licit and illicit use, and the issues of social and illegal drugs are so intermingled and complex that, more than ever, multi-disciplinary, inter-agency and international cooperation and collaboration are required. Without this there is no way to combat this endemic public health and social problem. In the absence of such a commitment, all the evidence that we have points to the fact that we are going to take the substance misuse/drug problem with us into the next millennium.

CHAPTER 5

Offences Relating to Importation and Exportation of Controlled Drugs

Relevant provisions of the Customs and Excise Management Act 1979 are set out in Appendix I.

The prohibitions

5.01 Section 68 of the Customs and Excise Management Act 1979 is modified in its application to precursors by the Controlled Drugs (Substances Useful for Manufacture) Regulations 1991 (S.I. 1991 No. 1285 set out in Appendix XXXV).

THE OFFENCES

Postal packets

5.03 The Postal Packets Regulations have been amended by the Postal Packets (Customs and Excise) (Amendment) Regulations 1992 (S.I. 1992 No. 3224). See Appendix II.

The decision in *Ciappara* was followed in *R.* v. *Mitchell* [1992] Crim.L.R. 594, C.A. Unsolicited receipt of drugs followed by knowing retention entitles a jury to convict of an offence against section 170(2).

Knowledge of the drugs

5.04 The decision in *Siracusa* (1990) 90 Cr.App.R. 340 was further explained in *R.* v. *Chandrakant Patel and others* (August 7, 1991, C.A., unreported) para. 10.09 *post*). The name of the drug in the indictment is not a material particular. The defendant must be proved to have conspired to import a drug of the same Class or a lesser Class.

Evidence of knowledge

5.06 In a case concerning a passenger in a car in which drugs had been concealed in the petrol tank, the Court of Appeal allowed the appeal. The only question was whether, by reason of his presence in the car, the jury could safely conclude that if the driver knew about the drugs then the appellant must know about them also. This was insufficient. *R.* v. *Suurmeijer* [1991] Crim.L.R. 773.

CHAPTER 6

Evidential and Procedural Provisions

PROCEDURE

Witness statements made outside the United Kingdom

6.11 The decision in *Bateman and Cooper* was reversed following a reference to the Court of Appeal by the Home Secretary under section 17(1)(*a*) of the Criminal Appeal Act 1968: *R.* v. *Bateman, Cooper and Davies* (1992) 94 Cr.App.R. 372. Even if the statement of a foreign witness is tendered at the committal proceedings it cannot be read at the trial. Section 3 of the Criminal Justice (International Co-operation) Act 1990 makes provision for obtaining evidence abroad but not for its admission in courts in the United Kingdom. The law requires amendment so that section 9 of the Criminal Justice Act 1967 specifically applies to statements of foreign witnesses where they do not contain a statutory declaration.

Foreign documents—copies
6.14 For the effect of a foreign supermarket receipt, see para. 6.15A.

SOME CASES ON EVIDENCE

6.15 The case of *Willis* was once again referred to by the Court of Appeal in *R.* v. *Morgan* [1993] Crim.L.R. 56 when it was held that it was right to allow the Crown to prove that the appellant had admitted she knew people who smoked cocaine and that she allowed it to be smoked in her house. She had been stopped with 227 grams of cocaine which she claimed had been planted on her. The passage complained of was relevant to prove that the appellant had a link with cocaine.

The decision in *Cooper* was relied on by the appellant in *McIntosh*, February 28, 1992, C.A., (briefly reported in [1992] Crim.L.R. 651) where a piece of paper bearing calculations of prices and weights was found up the chimney of the appellant's ex-wife's house, where he had been staying. The document was not in the appellant's handwriting. The court considered that the decision in *R.* v. *Lydon* (1987) 85 Cr.App.R. 221 was more apposite. The calculations were admissible. They were not hearsay but were real evidence. The court cited with approval the following passage from *Archbold: Criminal Pleading, Evidence and Practice*:

> "In order to put a document in evidence as 'real evidence' under this principle a sufficient foundation must be laid to link the defendant to the document. Thus, it is submitted, there must be prima facie evidence that he was the author of the document, or that he was in, or had been in possession or control of the document, or that he knew of the document or was in some other way connected with it." (1992 Edition, para. 9–6, p. 1443.)

The court also stated that where a document is sought to be introduced as part of the circumstantial evidence in the case rather than as the evidence of the truth of its contents, the question whether a sufficient link with the defendant has been established must be a question of fact and degree. Prima facie the fact that the appellant had lived in the house for the previous two months was a sufficient link. Ultimately, it should have been left to the jury to decide whether a sufficient link had been established.

This decision may be contrasted with that of the House of Lords in *R.* v. *Kearley* (para. 15.07 *post*) and of the Court of Appeal in *Howey* v. *Bradley* (1969) 114 S.J. 37, D.C. Calculations and conversions are frequently found in the vicinity of drug traffickers (as are scales). They are real evidence; a part of the process of trafficking.

The decision in the appeal of *R.* v. *Horne* [1992] Crim.L.R. 304, C.A., went the other way. In that case, the appellant had handed over suitcases containing drugs to a co-defendant who pleaded guilty. Pieces of paper containing calculations and references to the appellant and his sister were found at the co-defendant's flat. There was no evidence that the appellant had been in the flat. It was held that the provenance (link) of the documents fell far short of that which could render them admissible against the appellant. A re-trial was ordered but the prosecution failed to have the appellant re-arraigned within the statutory period of two months set by section 8 of the Criminal Appeal Act 1968 and the appellant was therefore entitled to a verdict of acquittal.

Section 24 Criminal Justice Act 1988

6.15A *R.* v. *Murphy, Wiseman and Mason* [1992] Crim.L.R. 883 concerned admissibility under section 24 of the Criminal Justice Act 1988. The appellants were accused of substituting cannabis resin for beer in packages bought in a Calais supermarket. In their van was a receipt from the Continent Hypermarket in Calais for, *inter alia*, four tubes of superglue. The Court of Appeal held that the receipt was admissible under section 24 of the Criminal Justice Act 1988 to prove the facts disclosed by it. Subsections (1)(i) and (ii) were satisfied and subsection (4) was not relevant.

CHAPTER 7

Powers of Detention and Search

Police and Criminal Evidence Act 1984

7.01 The Police and Criminal Evidence Act 1984 (Application to Customs and Excise) Order 1985 does not specifically apply section 66 (Codes of Practice) of PACE to the activities of Customs and Excise officers, but section 67(9) of PACE states:

> "(9) Persons other than police officers who are charged with the duty of investigating offences or charging offenders shall in the discharge of that duty have regard to any relevant provision of such a code."

In *R.* v. *Sanusi* [1992] Crim.L.R. 43, the Court of Appeal held that in the circumstances of the case, there had been such breaches of the Code (C: 3.1 and C: 3.2) as to lead to the exclusion of an interview conducted by Customs officers.

Customs officers have power to require information to be furnished concerning goods for which an entry is required (section 77). Persons entering or leaving the United Kingdom must answer questions with respect to their baggage (section 78(2)). It would appear, therefore, that there is no need to caution such a person before questioning him about his baggage.

DETENTION OF PERSONS

7.02 Where an arrested person was questioned in a hotel room and denied access to a solicitor there was a breach of section 30(10) of PACE and he should have been taken to a police station (or Customs office: Schedule 2 of the Order of 1985 set out in Appendix III). However, the interview was properly admitted, the trial judge having had regard to section 78 of PACE: *R.* v. *Kerawalla* [1991] Crim.L.R. 451.

CHAPTER 8

Penalties and Forfeiture

PENALTIES

8.01 Section 68 of the Customs and Excise Management Act 1979 is modified in its application to precursors by the Controlled Drugs (Substances Useful for Manufacture) Regulations 1991 (S.I. 1991 No. 1285, set out in Appendix XXXV.)

A reference by the Attorney-General to the Court of Appeal for the increase of a sentence under section 36 of the Criminal Justice Act 1988 cannot be made in the case of substantive offences because they are triable either way. Such a reference can be made in the case of conspiracy see, *e.g. Att.-Gen.'s Reference (No. 16 of 1991)* (1992) 13 Cr.App.R.(S.) 653.

With effect from October 1, 1992, the provisions relating to remission and release on licence are replaced by a new scheme: Criminal Justice Act 1991, Part II.

Drugs intended for use in a foreign country

8.03 With effect from October 1, 1992, the provisions relating to remission and release on licence are replaced by a new scheme: Criminal Justice Act 1991, Part II.

Guidelines on sentence

8.04 For an instance where a drug was below strength, see *R. v. French* (para. 18.06). Importers of heroin with a strength of 1 per cent. were sentenced to 12 years' imprisonment and eight years' respectively. It was held that the material was hardly recognisable as containing heroin and sentences of eight years and five years were substituted. *R. v. Afzal and Arshad* (1992) 13 Cr.App.R.(S.) 145.

Some sentences for importing which have been before the Court of Appeal

Drug and quantity	Value or remarks	Sentence	Reported
Heroin 600g (swallower)		8½ years	*The Times*, February 21, 1991
L.S.D. Conspiracy to import	£60,000–100,000	5 years	[1992] Crim.L.R. 836
Cocaine 20kg		life	(1992) 13 Cr.App.R.(S.) 702
694g (swallower)	Co-operated with customs	8 years	(1992) 13 Cr.App.R.(S.) 678
Organised importation (5.33kg)		14 years	(1992) 13 Cr.App.R.(S.) 583

Determining basis of sentence

8.07 Where a convicted importer claims that the drugs are intended for his own consumption, a Newton inquiry should be held (see para. 18.08 *post*) unless the suggestion is so absurd that it can be rejected out of hand. Such an importation is a more serious offence than simple possession of drugs but it nevertheless entails a considerable reduction in sentence. In the appeals of *Meah and Marlow* (1991) 92 Cr.App.R. 254 sentences of six years' and four years' imprisonment for importing heroin in condoms were reduced to three years and two years.

FORFEITURE

Forfeiture of money

8.11 The prescribed sum for section 25 is £10,000: Criminal Justice (International Co-operation) Act 1990 (Detention and Forfeiture of Drug Trafficking Cash) Order 1991 (S.I. 1991 No. 1816). In connection with applications under sections 25 or 26 see Magistrates' Courts (Detention and Forfeiture of Drug Trafficking Cash) Rules 1991 (S.I. 1991 No. 1923) (set out in Appendix XXXIII).

CHAPTER 9

Controlled Drugs and Their Classification

DEFINITION AND CLASSIFICATION

9.02 The Court of Appeal in its decision in *R. v. Chandrakant Patel and others* (August 7, 1991, C.A. unreported) concerning conspiracy to produce drugs, held that where all that is being considered in connection with an offence of conspiracy is prohibited drugs of the same class, the name of the drug in the Particulars of Offence is not a material particular. The court went on to say that if it was right, then it might be thought that the best course for the Crown to adopt was not to name the drug in the Particulars of Offence. The Crown did not agree. If the Crown was clear as to the drug involved, it should be identified.

This may indicate a new approach if the Crown is in difficulty in proving the exact nature of a drug but can prove that it comes within a Class that is prohibited.

Expert evidence

9.05 A case where the evidence of a supervising analyst was rejected is *R. v. Agritraders Ltd.* (November 17, 1981, C.A., unreported on this issue). The Court of Appeal held that it could not be concerned with the difficulties which face a prosecuting authority. The witness had not participated in the processes of analysis. His evidence dealt with his examination of the results and his critical assessment of the results with the aid of a spectrograph.

When an analysis is made in a laboratory and the result is not through a statutory provision produced in the form of what might be called a certificate of proof, oral evidence given by the person in overall charge of the making of that analysis, but who played no part in it, cannot be regarded as admissible evidence of the accuracy of it in the absence of testimony from the person of the manner in which it was done and to what effect.

Nature of drugs proved by inference

9.06A   The effect of the decision in *R*. v. *Hunt* [1987] A.C. 352, H.L.
(see para. 19.03 of main work) is not to require scientific evidence to be
adduced in every case in order to identify a prohibited drug. However,
the prosecution must establish the identity of the drug with sufficient
certainty to achieve the standard of proof required in a criminal case: *R*.
v. *Hill* (November 4, 1992, C.A., unreported). The relevant part of the
decision concerned Count 12 of an indictment charging the supply of
cannabis resin. The court was not referred to the decision in *R*. v.
Chandrakant Patel and others (see para. 10.09 *post*). The appellant was
observed supplying "a small dark object" and, five months later, cannabis
resin was found at his girlfriend's home. The court considered the
decision in *R*. v. *Best and others* (1979) 70 Cr.App.R. 21 (see para. 9.03 of
main work) and appeared to be influenced by the fact that the charge
specified cannabis resin alone. It held that the descriptions given by the
police officers of what changed hands were insufficient to justify a certain
inference that it was cannabis resin.

CHAPTER 10

Production and Supply

THE PROHIBITION

10.01   For the *mens rea* required for a conspiracy to supply or to produce see para. 10.09 *post*.

Production of "Crack"
10.02A   The Court of Appeal had to consider the question of whether free-basing (converting cocaine hydrochloride into cocaine) amounted to the production of a drug. The appellant contended that altering a drug listed in Part I of Schedule 2 to the Act into another form of that drug also listed or included in Part I could not amount to production. The court referred to section 37 and to the different properties of the two "substances"; cocaine hydrochloride is water soluble and has a high melting point whereas free-base is not soluble in water and vaporises easily. It held that the conversion of one form of a Class A drug into another form of the same genus may amount to production. The conversion of the salt into the base (not by manufacture of cultivation "but by other means") with physical and chemical features different from the cocaine hydrochloride from which it sprung amounts to production: *R. v. Russell* (1992) 94 Cr.App.R. 351.

Production of MDMA
10.02B   MDMA (or Ecstasy) is defined in paragraph (*c*) of Part I of Schedule 2 of the Act. It is structurally derived from N-alkyl-alpha-methylphenethylamine by substitution in the ring with an alkylenedioxy substituent. In the first prosecution for producing MDMA, it was unsuccessfully argued by the defence that paragraph (*c*) describes processes rather than an end product. It was contended that it is not an almost passive description of a molecule, it is a description of the manner of its achievement. The method actually prescribes the end result. It controls the legality or the illegality of the end product. (If this argument were correct, it would mean that in a case of simple possession it would be necessary to prove the process of production.) However, His Honour

Judge Watts sitting at Acton Crown Court in effect ruled that paragraph (*c*) should be construed as a definition of an end product rather than of the process by which it had been made. He accepted that the formula of MDMA was within the chemical definition in paragraph (*c*). The Court of Appeal upheld this ruling. They held that the words of paragraph (*c*) are not to be interpreted by giving them their ordinary and natural meanings. The principle of interpretation, therefore, being that the words must be given their ordinary and natural meaning to a person qualified to understand them, *i.e.* a chemist. The words define controlled drugs by describing the structure of their molecules: *R.* v. *Couzens and Frankel* [1992] Crim.L.R. 822.

The meaning of "supply"

10.03 The other person may be a person named in a different count of the same indictment. *R.* v. *Connelly* [1992] Crim.L.R. 296.

Offer to supply

10.04 The offer completes the offence whether or not the offeror intends or is able to supply the drug. *R.* v. *Mitchell* [1992] Crim.L.R. 723 and *R.* v. *Goddard* [1992] Crim.L.R. 588.

Jurisdiction: England and Scotland

10.05A Two defendants in England supplied seven kilograms of cannabis to a co-defendant who then took it to Scotland for distribution. So far as one of the defendants was concerned, there was no evidence that he knew the drugs were going to Scotland. They were convicted in Scotland of being concerned in the supply of drugs, together with other defendants, at locations in England and Scotland. It was conceded by their counsel that there was sufficient evidence for them to be convicted in England. They appealed on the grounds that in the absence of section 148 of the Customs and Excise Management Act 1979 (set out in Appendix I of the main work), Scottish courts only have jurisdiction over offences under the Misuse of Drugs Act 1971 when they are committed in Scotland.

In his judgment, the Lord Justice General cited *Kerr* (see para. 10.05 of main work) as to the wide scope of section 4(3). He held that all who participate in the chain of supply are subject to the jurisdiction of the courts of the place in the United Kingdom where the chain comes to an end. The interests of justice are best served by trying all those who participated in the chain together in the same court rather than separately accordingly to the parts of the United Kingdom where their activities occurred. It is logical to look to the place where the mischief would take place as the place where jurisdiction can be established against all the participants: *Clements* v. *H.M. Advocate*, 1991 S.L.T. 388.

SUPPLY AND MANSLAUGHTER

10.08   The facts of *Austin* appear to have been repeated in the case of *R.* v. *Clarke* [1992] T.L.R. 35 where a sentence of five years' imprisonment was reduced to three-and-a-half years.

CONSPIRACY TO PRODUCE

Mens rea of conspirators

10.09A   The decision in *R.* v. *Siracusa* (1990) 90 Cr.App.R. 340 (*ante*, para. 5.04 of main work) was relied on by the appellants in *R.* v. *Chandrakant Patel and others* (August 7, 1991, C.A., unreported) who had been convicted of conspiracies to produce amphetamine and to supply amphetamine. They criticised the trial judge who had directed the jury:

> "If it is proved to your satisfaction that he knew the chemicals, or some of them, were for illegal drug production, but it has not been proved that he knew it was for the production of amphetamine sulphate, you will then have to decide whether his knowledge of the scheme was sufficiently close that it can properly be said that he attached himself to that scheme and not to something different."

The Court of Appeal held that such a direction was apposite, provided that it was made clear to the jury that the defendant must have believed that the scheme referred to was the manufacture of a drug of the same Class or a lesser Class. The name of the drug in the indictment is not a material averment.

The position was summarised by the court:

> "If a defendant is charged with an offence of conspiracy and the Particulars of Offence identify the drug involved then:
>
> (i) a defendant will not be guilty of that offence unless the jury are satisfied that he knew that the drugs to which the conspiracy related were prohibited drugs. If the jury are so satisfied then he will only be entitled to be acquitted, so far as his intent is concerned, if the jury consider that, although he agreed to join the conspiracy, he may have mistakenly believed that the conspiracy related to a different drug from that named in the Particulars of Offence and that different drug is of a Class, the maximum punishment in relation to which (for the substantive offence) is less than that for drugs of the Class specified in the Particulars of Offence. Thus if a person enters into a conspiracy believing it concerns cannabis (Class B) he will not be guilty of an offence charging him with

being a party to a conspiracy concerning heroin (Class A). If he mistakenly thought that he was joining a conspiracy to commit a graver offence his mistake would not be as to a material feature of the offence, in other words he believed the drug involved was heroin when in fact it was cannabis;

(ii) a defendant will be guilty of the offence if he joined the conspiracy alleged in the mistaken belief it involved a drug which, while different from, belongs to the same Class as the drug named in the Particulars of Offence;

(iii) a defendant will be guilty if he joins the conspiracy knowing that prohibited drugs are involved but without knowing what drugs are involved. In such a situation he would in fact have agreed to be a party to the conspiracy irrespective of what drugs are involved."

Substances useful for manufacture of controlled drugs

10.10   Schedule 2 has been amended by the addition of 10 substances with effect from January 1, 1993. (The Criminal Justice (International Co-operation) Act 1990, set out in Appendix XV to the main work.)

PRECURSOR AND ESSENTIAL CHEMICALS NOW LISTED IN TABLE I
AND TABLE II OF ANNEX AND SCHEDULE 2 OF THE ACT

Table I

Chemicals	Illicit use	Legitimate use
N-Acetyl Anthranilic acid	A solid powder used in producing N-acetyl anthranilic acid (methaqualone precursor)	Manufacturing plastics, chemicals and pharmaceuticals
Ephedrine	A solid powder used in producing methamphetamine	Manufacturing bronchodilators
Ergonovine (Ergometrine)	A solid powder used in producing LSD; also a precursor of lysergic acid	Medicinally as a uterine stimulant and cerebral vasodilator
Ergotamine	A solid powder used in producing LSD; also a precursor of lysergic acid	Medicinally as a uterine stimulant and cerebral vasodilator

Chemicals	Illicit use	Legitimate use
Isosafrole	A liquid with odour of anise used to manufacture the hallucinogen MDMA, etc.	Used for flavouring and in the fragrance industry
Lysergic acid	Crystalline material used in production of LSD	Used in various organic syntheses
3, 4-Methylenedioxy-phenyl-2-propanone	A liquid used in producing MDA, N-hydroxy MDA, MDMA and MDE	Laboratory analytical reagent
1-phenyl-2-propanone (P2P)	Liquid used as precursor in the synthesis of amphetamine, methampethamine and analogues	Manufacture of pharmaceutical products
Piperonal	Colourless crystals used for production of MDMA, etc.	Used for flavouring and in the fragrances industry
Pseudoephedrine	A solid powder used in producing methamphetamine	Manufacturing bronchodilators
Safrole	A colourless liquid used to manufacture the hallucinogen MDMA, etc.	Used for flavouring and in the fragrance industry

Table II

Chemicals	Illicit use	Legitimate use
Acetic anhydride	A liquid used in producing heroin from morphine, N-acetyl-anthranilic acid (methaqualone and mecloqualone precursor) and P2P (methamphetamine and amphetamine precursor)	Acetylation, dehydration, manufacturing dyes, plastics, herbicides, fragrances and pharmaceuticals
Acetone	A solvent used in converting cocaine base to cocaine hydrochloride	Manufacturing plastics, paints, agricultural products, etc.
Anthranilic acid	A solid powder used in producing N-acetyl-anthranilic acid (methaqualone precursor)	Manufacturing dyes, pigments, pharmaceuticals, lubricants and agricultural chemicals
Ethyl ether	A solvent used in converting cocaine base to cocaine hydrochloride	Manufacturing munitions, plastics, and as an anaesthetic in surgery
Hydrochloric acid	Colourless, highly corrosive liquid used in the refinement of cocaine	Manufactured in great quantity (15,000 metric tons p.a.) for use as an industrial catalyst and solvent
Methyl ethyl ketone	A solvent used in converting cocaine hydrochloride	Manufacturing coatings, decreasing agents, lacquers, resins and smokeless powders

Chemicals	Illicit use	Legitimate use
Phenylacetic acid	Powder used in the syntheses of P2P, amphetamine and methamphetamine	Manufacture of pharmaceutical products, perfumes and flavours
Piperidine	A liquid used in producing phencyclidine (PCP)	Solvent and curing agent, catalyst and ingredient in oils and fuels
Potassium permanganate	A dark purple crystalline solid used in converting coca paste to cocaine base	Bleaching applications, disinfectants, antibacterials, antifungal agents
Sulphuric acid	A colourless, oily, highly corrosive liquid used in the extraction of cocaine	Manufactured in enormous quantities (80,000 metric tons p.a.) for manufacture of fertilisers, explosives, paper, glue, battery fluids, etc.
Toluene	Solvent used in the conversion of cocaine base to cocaine hydrochloride and in the production of other controlled substances	Manufacture of exploring dyes, coatings, other organic materials; industrial gasoline additive; conversion to benzene

See also Table 3.1 on p.51 of the main work.

The Controlled Drugs (Substances Useful for Manufacture) Regulations 1991 as amended (S.I. 1991 No. 1285) and Council Regulation 3677/90/EEC (set out in Appendices XXXV and XXXVI respectively) concern licensing documentation and monitoring of trade in precursors.

CHAPTER 11

Possession and Possession with Intent to Supply

INTENT TO SUPPLY

Evidence of intent to supply

11.12   Where the appellant was indicted with possessing specified drugs with intent to supply, the jury were entitled to consider surveillance evidence if they were sure that it could be inferred from it that supplies of unspecified drugs had been made by the appellant on earlier occasions. *R.* v. *Hill* (1993) 96 Cr.App.R. 456.

Some Cases on Evidence

Secondary evidence of exhibits

15.03 Part of the exhibits consisting of 900 grams of cannabis resin disappeared during the course of the trial. This was not an irregularity which was material to the outcome of the case: *R.* v. *Hooker and Boyce* (April 12, 1991, C.A., unreported).

Similar fact evidence

15.04 The decision in *R.* v. *Wells* may need reconsideration in the light of the reasoning of the House of Lords in *D.P.P.* v. *P.* (1991) 93 Cr.App.R. 267.

Interviews—influence of drugs or of withdrawal symptoms

15.05 The following submission has been made by "Justice" (the British section of the International Commission of Jurists) to the Home Office.

"Proposed addition to Code C: Code of Practice for the Detention, Treatment and Questioning of Persons by Police Officers to deal with persons under the influence of drugs (or drink) or suffering from withdrawal symptoms.
The following paragraph should be substituted for Note 12B:-
'*Note 12B*   A person who appears to be unfit through drink or drugs or to be suffering from illness, including symptoms of withdrawl from addictive drugs, shall not be interviewed unless a police surgeon has certified that he is fit to be interviewed. Such a certificate should state the period within which a person will be fit for interview'.

Explanation
It is felt that para. C12.3 together with Note C12B does not provide sufficient protection for persons suffering from illness, especially from withdrawal symptoms. When persons are examined, the police surgeon usually restricts himself to certifying that they are fit to be detained. Whilst it is understood that in the Metropolitan Police Area such a certificate does deal with fitness to be interviewed, this practice should be made general and compulsory. The certificate should state the period for which it is valid for two reasons:
    1. Interviews are often delayed to suit the convenience of officers. It is felt

that an interview should be commenced within a reasonable period after the medical examination.
2. In the case of withdrawal symptoms (or of such illnesses as migraine) it may be necessary to prescribe medicine which will require a period to elapse before it takes effect."

Undercover operations
15.06A   See the contrasting decisions in *R.* v. *Bryce* [1992] Crim.L.R. 728 and *R.* v. *Christou and Wright* (1992) 95 Cr.App.R. 264.

Evidence from telephone calls and visitors

15.07   The decision in *Kearley* was reversed by the House of Lords (1992) 95 Cr.App.R. 88. It was held that the rule against hearsay does, indeed, prevent the words of telephone callers being used to prove that the appellant had, in the past, supplied drugs or that the speaker believed that the appellant at present had drugs in his possession and was willing to supply them.

The decision of the House of Lords in *Kearley* was cited unsuccessfully in the appeal of *Warner and Jones* (1993) 96 Cr.App.R. 324. In that case, evidence had been given under section 74 of PACE of the drugs convictions of callers at the appellants' premises in order to prove that they were supplying drugs. The Court of Appeal held that the evidence of convictions did not amount to hearsay; it established the character of the people whom the defendants and their accomplices were letting into the house. It was relevant to the nature of the transactions which they were taking place. The judge in summing-up should have analysed the issue to the evidence was relevant.

It is admissible for a police officer to assert that the persons to whom the appellant passed packages were known to the police as heroin users. Where such evidence is objected to by the defence, it must be analysed. If it was based on hearsay, it would be excluded. If the officer had first-hand knowledge of the alleged recipient being in possession of drugs or receiving treatment for addiction, then it might be admitted, subject to the judge's discretion to exclude it under section 78 of PACE. Convictions would be admissible under section 74: *R.* v. *Rothwell, The Times*, April 27, 1993.

The Court of Appeal considered the effect of sections 1 and 9 of the Interception of Communications Act 1985 in the unsuccessful appeals of *Effik and Mitchell* (1992) 95 Cr.App.R. 427. Evidence of calls on a cordless telephone between a third party and the appellants, intercepted by the police without a warrant under the Act, was admitted at the trial. It was assumed for the purpose of the appeal that such interception amounted to an offence against section 1. It was nevertheless held that the general rule applied that all logically probative evidence is admissible. The express terms of section 9 did not provide that no evidence obtained as a result of an interception could be admitted. It seemed that consistent with the police underlying section 9, it would usually be perfectly proper for the Crown simply to decline to say whether a warrant was or was not issued. There was no basis for excluding the evidence under section 78 of PACE. What mattered was the quality and content of the records. (See also *D.P.P.* v. *McGladrigan* [1991] Crim.L.R. 851, a case concerning a breathalyser following an unlawful arrest.)

The Interception of Communications Act 1985 was again before the Court of Appeal in *R.* v. *Preston and others* (1992) 95 Cr.App.R. 355 a case where a warrant had been issued. Evidence of the making of telephone calls, but not of their content, was adduced by the Crown. The Court of Appeal held that the purpose of a warrant was not to obtain evidence for use in court and that it is normally not possible to adduce any evidence obtained as a result of an interception to which the Act applies. The court went on to give guidance as to what should be disclosed to the defence and the application of the Attorney-General's Guidelines.

The prosecution was rightly allowed to prove the previous convictions of visitors under section 74 of PACE. The previous convictions were relevant to an issue in the proceedings, namely the nature of the transactions in which the defendants were taking part: *R.* v. *Warner*, *The Times*, November 16, 1992, C.A.

Privilege of informers, etc.

Observation posts
15.10   Putting observation posts in the same category as informers is not an unwarranted extension of the courts' protection given to police sources of information: *R.* v. *Hewitt*, *R.* v. *Davis* (1992) 95 Cr.App.R. 81. Both informers and the providers of observation posts provide the police with indispensable assistance in the detection of crime. The Court of Appeal approved the following directions:

The judge (trial of Hewitt):

> "That has been a handicap to them and you have to give great consideration to that and in considering the evidence you have to always remember that handicap (if I may call it that) which has been placed on the defence and how important it is, in the light of all the evidence. For example—I say for example—you might form the view that the prosecution evidence was so strong that the handicap mattered little. On the other hand, you might find that the handicap, coupled with your view of the rest of the evidence produced a situation where you could not be satisfied that the prosecution had proved their case on any of those four cannabis charges. Bear that in mind, members of the jury. It is a handicap and it is an important handicap. It does not mean you

cannot bring in a verdict of guilty, but in considering the evidence you have to always remember that and keep it in the forefront of your mind."

The recorder (trial of Davis):

"Consequently, people who help the police in that way are entitled to the reassurance that their identities will not be disclosed.

Well, there is the balance and how the law resolves the difficult balance between two conflicting public interests, and as I say this particular one is not criticised. The effect of the application of the rule, though, does have the effect that you are to some extent limited, as Miss Forshall has pointed out, it must be acknowledged, but you are limited to this extent that the observing evidence, the evidence of the two officers, Woman Police Constable Sharma and Police Constable Chadwick, cannot be tested to the same extent as it would normally be, and you have to rely upon what evidence you have heard about it from them (and I will remind you of it shortly), and to that extent the defendant is inhibited in the presentation of his case."

R. v. *Johnson* and *R.* v. *Hewitt*; *R.* v. *Davis* were approved and followed by the Divisional Court in *Blake and Austin* v. *D.P.P.* [1993] Crim.L.R. 283. (The case concerned acts of indecent behaviour.) The court again held that there was no essential difference between informers and the providers of observation posts.

CHAPTER 16

Special Provisions Relating to Offences

Assisting and inducing offences outside the United Kingdom

16.02 Section 20 creates a substantive offence *Chief Constable of Hampshire* v. *Mace* (1987) 84 Cr.App.R. 40; *R.* v. *McShane* (1977) 66 Cr.App.R. 97. If the offence "aimed at" would be punishable under the provisions of the corresponding law, then it is an offence to conspire or to attempt in the United Kingdom to assist or induce the commission of such an offence abroad. (Section 1 Criminal Law Act 1977 and section 1 Criminal Attempts Act 1981.) The wording of section 20 is not apt to cover a conspiracy in the United Kingdom for the conspirators themselves to commit an offence abroad.

CHAPTER 17

Powers of Search and Arrest

Obstruction

17.03 Obstruction is not an arrestable offence: *Edwards* v. *D.P.P., The Times*, March 29, 1993.

POWERS OF SEARCH

Power to search premises

17.05 Section 32(2) of PACE empowers a constable to enter premises in which an arrested person was immediately before he was arrested for evidence relating to the offence for which he was arrested. Subsection (6) only permits such a search if the constable has reasonable grounds for believing that there is such evidence on the premises. The Court of Appeal held that following a lawful arrest in the street of a person allegedly possessing drugs, a constable is entitled to enter premises which the person is known to have been in shortly before in order to search for evidence which might support the allegation: *R.* v. *Beckford* (1992) 94 Cr.App.R. 43.

Evidence obtained by illegal search

17.06 The Court of Appeal in *R.* v. *Beckford* (1992) 94 Cr.App.R. 43 approved the following passage from *Jones* v. *Owen* (1870) 34 J.P. 759:

> ". . . it would be a dangerous obstacle to the administration of justice if we were to hold, because evidence was obtained by illegal means, it could not be used against a party charged with an offence."

POWERS OF ARREST

17.07 Section 30 of PACE (arrest elsewhere than at police station) was

considered by the Court of Appeal in relation to subsequent searches of
the appellant's two flats. This was held to be justified under subsection
(10). Parts of his interrogation during the searches were properly
admitted, other facts were excluded. However the court warned that
section 30(10) did not give the police and Customs carte blanche to
conduct interviews which ought properly to be conducted in a police
station: *R. v. Khan* [1993] Crim.L.R. 54.

TREATMENT, SEARCHES ETC. OF DETAINED PERSONS

17.11 Application of Codes to PACE

(a) *Cautions*
   A. confirmed that a cigarette containing cannabis had been thrown out
of the window of his car. He was cautioned. Two minutes later heroin was
found in the car and he was questioned without a further caution. The
Court of Appeal held that the first caution was apt to cover further
discoveries in the car: *R. v. Oni* [1992] Crim.L.R. 183. There was no
breach of the Code of Practice C.10.1.

(b) *Questioning during search*
   Police raided a flat and found cannabis. They interviewed the
defendant forthwith. He declined to sign the record. At the police station
he denied that the interview had taken place. At the trial the following
objections were raised:

   (1) no contemporaneous record had been made;
   (2) the police had delayed taking the defendant to the police station
        and failed to record the delay;
   (3) the defendant was not offered a solicitor at the flat.

   The judge held that there were no breaches of the Code, but that if
there were, there was no unfairness sufficient to lead to exclusion under
section 78 of PACE.
   The Court of Appeal was inclined to think that there was a breach of
section 30 of PACE (to be taken to a police station as soon as practicable
after arrest) but that the judge had exercised his discretion to admit the
evidence correctly: *R. v. Keane* [1992] Crim.L.R. 306. (See also para.
17.07 *ante*.)

CHAPTER 18

Penalties

PUNISHMENT

18.01   A reference by the Attorney-General to the Court of Appeal for the increase of a sentence under section 36 of the Criminal Justice Act 1988 cannot be made in the case of substantive offences because they are triable either way. Such a reference can be made in the case of conspiracy see, *e.g. Att.-Gen.'s Reference (No. 16 of 1991)* (1992) 13 Cr.App.R.(S.) 653.

GUIDELINES ON SENTENCE

Drug and offence	Sentence	Reported
Heroin Conspiracy to supply	10 years	*Att.-Gen.'s Reference (No. 16 of 1991)* (1992) 13 Cr.App.R. (S.) 653
Cocaine Large scale supply Retail of "crack"	7 years 4 years	[1991] Crim.L.R. 721 (1992) 13 Cr.App.R.(S.) 356
LSD 20 doses	18 months' Y.C.	(1992) 13 Cr.App.R.(S.) 504
MDMA (Ecstasy) Experimental production (another)	9 years 6 years	[1992] T.L.R. 203
Methylamphetamine Large scale production (pleaded guilty)	12 years	[1992] Crim.L.R. 675
Cannabis Supply as retailer (730 grams)	2 years	(1992) 13 Cr.App.R.(S.) 127

Drug and offence	Sentence	Reported
Possession with intent (1410 grams) had involved young son in offence	5 years	[1991] Crim.L.R. 720
Possession with intent (29.6 grams)	3 months' Y.C.	(1992) 13 Cr.App.R.(S.) 262
Production (3 plants)	3 months	(1992) 13 Cr.App.R.(S.) 20
Possession of 9 grams	1 month consecutive to other offences	April 10, 1991, C.A.
Acid house party Conspiracy to supply Classes A and B	6 years	May 3, 1991, C.A.
Magic mushrooms Producing by drying	6 months immediate	October 14, 1991, C.A.
(another)	18 months suspended	

Mitigation

18.06 (3) *Entrapment*. Reductions of one-third to their sentences were allowed where two brothers were involved in supplying a large quantity of amphetamine to an undercover police officer: *R.* v. *Bigley, The Times*, September 22, 1992, C.A. See also *R.* v. *Mackey and Shaw* [1992] Crim.L.R. 602 where a sentence was reduced from seven to six years.

(8) *AIDS*. The defendant had a short life-expectancy owing to AIDS. Charges of possession of heroin with intent to supply and simple possession of heroin and cannabis were therefore ordered to remain on the file. Thereafter, he was twice arrested in possession of heroin. The original charges were re-activated and he was sentenced to four years' imprisonment. The Court of Appeal had regard to the fact that in DTOA proceedings, it had been found that his benefits from drug trafficking amounted to £60,000. A plea for his release so that he could die with dignity was rejected: *R.* v. *Stark* (1992) 13 Cr.App.R.(S.) 548.

Addiction

Probation with condition of treatment
18.07A Schedule 1A of the Powers of Criminal Courts Act 1973 was inserted by section 9(2) of the Criminal Justice Act 1991. Paragraph 6 of Schedule 1A is set out in Appendix XXVI *post*. This provision offers a

vital opportunity to defence counsel to endeavour to keep out of prison, not only drug offenders, but persons convicted of other offences where drug dependency caused or contributed to the offence. It must go some way to reduce the severity of the doctrine that a need to obtain drugs is no mitigation of offences of dishonesty. It is the first time that specific provision has been made in the criminal law for the treatment of drug addicts.

The provision will only lead to a significant fall in the use of imprisonment if sentencers can be persuaded to regard a reduction in the amount of illegal drugs consumed or a less frequent recourse to illegal drugs as representing a real effort to reform rather than as recidivism. Harm reduction should be the realistic aim of the sentencer. Complete abstinence must be a long term rather than an immediate objective.

The court must be satisfied that the defendant is dependent on drugs (or alcohol) or that he has a propensity towards the misuse of drugs (sub-paragraph (9)), and that his dependency (or propensity) requires or may be susceptible to treatment. If that condition is satisfied the probation order may include a requirement for treatment under the direction of a person having the necessary qualifications or experience (sub-paragraph (2)). The treatment may be residential, or at a specified institution or under the direction of a qualified person. In each case the institution or person must be specified in the order (sub-paragraph (3)). The court must be satisfied that arrangements have been made for the specified treatment before the probation order is made (sub-paragraph (4)).

It follows that a qualified or experienced person must have made a report assessing the defendant and made provisional arrangements before the court can exercise its powers under paragraph 6 (sub-paragraph (4)). The qualifications or experience are not defined and it follows that medical qualifications are not necessarily required. A pre-sentence report from a probation officer will be required. It is likely that the probation officer will use his knowledge and expertise to refer the defendant to an appropriate agency although there is nothing to prevent a defendant or his solicitors obtaining a report and a placement. If the treatment is to be at the expense of the defendant or his family the latter procedure will be the more appropriate.

Sub-paragraph (6) may require interpretation by the Court of Appeal since the wording does not sit well with that of sub-paragraph (3). The former gives the court power to order one of three kinds of treatment whereas the latter empowers the specified person to alter the institution specified. Only one of the specified forms of treatment allows for specification of a person so that if an institution was specified in the order there would not appear to be a specified person who could alter the specified institution. (Schedule 1A does not apply to supervision orders.)

The agency will need to assess the defendant's needs, supply information as to the appropriate treatment and what treatment it can offer and give some sort of prognosis. A great deal will depend on this assessment. In time courts will come to rely on their local agencies provided they confine their prognosis to achievable goals. The requirement will not itself set out the content and nature of the treatment to be suffered by the defendant. There is no power to require the agency to make any progress reports to the court but the supervising probation officer will need to be informed if the defendant does not attend for treatment or if he leaves an institution prematurely. The probation officer will need to refer the breach of the order to the court.

CHAPTER 25

Extradition and Drug Trafficking

Conventions

25.02   The Vienna Convention was ratified by the United Kingdom on June 28, 1991 and came into force for the United Kingdom on September 26, 1991 (Cm. 1927).

The Extradition (Drug Trafficking) Order 1991 ((S.I. 1991 No. 1701) set out in Appendix XXIIA) makes provision for extradition with respect to countries who are parties to the Vienna Convention but with which no general extradition arrangements have been made.

Drafting the Charge

GENERAL

Duplicity

27.03 The appellants were charged in 11 counts with being concerned in the unlawful supply of heroin. Each count related to a specific day and nine counts charged two or more of the appellants with being concerned with the supply on that date. The Court of Appeal held that the activities of the appellants all took place within a confined location, within a confined time, and the supply in all cases was of heroin. The question whether the criminal enterprise formed part of what was in reality one activity was a question of fact and degree. The submission that the indictment was bad for duplicity was rejected. *R.* v. *Fyffe and others* [1992] Crim.L.R. 442.

Alternatives
27.04 *Best* was followed in *R.* v. *Mitchell* [1992] Crim.L.R. 723.

MATERIAL PARTICULARS

27.11 The exact nature of the drug is not a material particular although its classification is. If the Crown is clear as to the drug involved, it should be named: *R.* v. *Chandrakant Patel and others* (August 7, 1991, C.A., unreported) discussed in para. 10.09A *ante*.

CHAPTER 29

Introductory

Interpretation

29.01 The confiscation provisions of the Act are penal and must be construed in favour of the defendant: *R. v. Chapman* [1991] T.L.R. 518. (But see section 7(2) of the Criminal Justice Act 1993 which will insert a new section 1(7A) in the Drug Trafficking Offences Act 1986 applying the civil standard of proof, set out in Appendix XXXVII.)

RUN THROUGH OF PROCEDURE

(a) Preservation and disclosure

29.05 (See also Chap. 31.) Where a person has been charged with a drug trafficking offence, or is to be so charged, (section 7 DTOA) application can be made to the High Court for a restraint order or a charging order. Where a restraint order has been made, the High Court may at any time appoint a receiver (section 8(6)). When a restraint order is made, the High Court can also order the defendant to swear an affidavit disclosing the value, nature and whereabouts of his assets worldwide: *Re T., The Times*, May 19, 1992, C.A., see para. 30.04.

Proceedings are initiated, varied and concluded by way of an application to a judge of the Queen's Bench Division in chambers. Proceedings are issued through the Crown Office and heard only in London.

But see the new section 1A (postponed determinations) inserted by Criminal Justice Act 1993, s.8.

(b) Making of confiscation order

(See also Chap. 30.) Before or after conviction, the prosecution may serve a statement under section 3 of the DTOA. It must comply with rule 25A of the Crown Court (Amendment) Rules 1986 (set out in Appendix XIII of the main work). Except in the simplest cases, it is unlikely that any further steps will be taken under section 3 before conviction (see para.

30.04). Isleworth Crown Court has issued a Practice Direction (set out in Appendix XXVII, *post*).

After conviction the case is likely to be remanded in order for the procedures under section 3 to be carried out. Sentence must be postponed. It is important for the prosecution to activate section 3(2) so as to obtain a requirement that the defendant indicates to what extent he accepts allegations in the prosecution statement and, so far as he does not accept any such allegation, to indicate what matters he relies on, but see now section 10 of the Criminal Justice Act 1993 which inserts a new section 3A into the 1986 Act, set out in Appendix XXXVII. (See especially *Re T.* discussed in para. 30.04 *post.*)

Before he can sentence the defendant, the judge must:

(1) Determine whether the defendant has benefited from drug trafficking, and, if he has:
    (a) the value of his benefits;
    (b) the value of property available to satisfy a confiscation order;
(2) make the order; or
(3) he may issue a certificate as to any matter relevant for determining the amount that may be realised and he must issue a certificate if the amount realised is less than the value of the benefits (section 4(2)).

When he makes a confiscation order, the judge must specify which statutory assumptions he has made and set out the payments and rewards he finds have been received by the defendant, and the value of the realisable assets, in such a manner, that the Court of Appeal will know exactly what his findings were.

(c) Enforcement

(See also para. 30.08, Chaps. 32 and 33 and see s.6(7) inserted by Criminal Justice Act 1993, s.13, set out in Appendix XXXVII.) A confiscation order operates *in personam* and a defendant has a choice of how he realises assets to raise the total sum ordered to be confiscated. The judge will order that the sum shall be paid to a specified magistrates' court, he will specify a period or periods within which it must be paid and must specify a period of imprisonment to be served consecutively in default of payment. The defendant does not, however, necessarily have the choice of paying or serving the extra sentence (para. 30.08).

Enforcement falls to the clerk to the justices unless the prosecutor applies to the High Court for the appointment of a receiver (para. 32.01).

(d) Appeal or variation

A confiscation order is part of the sentence of the court and an appeal lies to the Court of Appeal (para. 30.12).

The defendant may apply to the High Court for a certificate that the property available is inadequate for the full satisfaction of a confiscation order (para. 33.01).

The prosecution may apply to the High Court where there is a certificate that the value of the assets is less than the value of the profits, for a certificate that the amount that may be realised is in fact greater. (See para. 33.04 and sections 5A, 5B and 5C, inserted by Criminal Justice Act 1993, s.12, set out in Appendix XXXVII.)

The maximum periods are set out in section 31(3A) of the Powers of Criminal Courts Act 1973.

CHAPTER 30

Confiscation Orders

KEY TO PROCEDURE

5. & 6. The period to be served in default of payment should be imposed after the imposition of the sentence for the offence since it is expressed as consecutive to the sentence.

Making the order

30.01 Section 1A (to be inserted by section 8 of the Criminal Justice Act 1993, set out in Appendix XXXVII, *post*) will allow the court to postpone its determinations, but nevertheless proceed to sentence (subsection (7)). The sentence may not include a fine or other financial penalty (subsection (9)). It may also postpone its determination pending an appeal against conviction. The maximum period of postponement is six months from the date of conviction or three months from the determination of the appeal.

Section 14 of the Criminal Justice Act 1993 will add a new section 4A to make provision for the situation where a convicted person dies or absconds before sentence. A new section 19A, inserted by section 15 of the Criminal Justice Act 1993, will make provision for compensation for a defendant who is subsequently acquitted.

Amount to be recovered

30.02 Where the court finds that there is nothing to be realised it will make a nominal order (section 4(3) as to be amended by section 7(3) of the Criminal Justice Act 1993). This will make it possible for the position to be reconsidered if assets are later discovered (section 16 of the Criminal Justice (International Co-operation) Act 1990). It will only be effective where the court has made an assessment of the value of the defendant's proceeds.

Although expenses are not deducted when arriving at the value of the benefit it is nevertheless logical, when estimating the property available as a result of selling drugs, to make some allowance for expenses that must necessarily have been involved in the operation. *R.* v. *Comiskey* (1991) 93 Cr.App.R. 227, 232.

The amount to be realised by the sale of a property means the amount that will be realised from the sale of the property less the costs of the sale such as commission to estate agents, legal costs, VAT and so on. *R.* v. *Cramer* (1992) 13 Cr.App.R.(S.) 390.

Mortgages

30.02A Where property has been mortgaged, the mortgage is an obligation having priority within the meaning of section 5(3)(*b*). It has to be deducted before the amount that can be realised is arrived at. *R.* v. *MacDonald* (October 11, 1990, C.A., unreported). It obviously cannot have been part of the proceeds where it is a normal loan from a bank or a building society. (See also para. 30.05 *post.*)

Gifts caught by the Act

30.03 In his judgment in *Re B.* (May 13, 1991, D.C., unreported) (Crown Office) Henry J. had occasion to consider the effect of section 5(10) on property transferred to his wife by a convicted drug trafficker. She had applied to the High Court under section 11(8). (Since there is no provision for an interested person to be heard at the Crown Court, the wife was not bound by the findings of the trial judge in making the confiscation order.) He observed that the Act makes no special provision to protect the rights under matrimonial legislation of the criminal's wife to an interest in the matrimonial home. The wife has to show that she has an interest in property otherwise than by a gift as defined in the Act. A gift caught by the Act is not only a gratuitous transfer of property but also the transfer for good consideration where that transfer is at an undervalue. The courts must concern themselves with the adequacy of consideration.

Whether or not a contract is legally enforceable matters not if the property is actually transferred. The question is whether the transferee gave valuable consideration. The judge said:

> "If the consideration she provided was not money but the provision of services worth money, then, equally, I do not see why that should not be valuable consideration within the meaning of the Act, once the property had been transferred to her. But where in an unenforceable domestic arrangement the consideration is in the form of payment by the drug trafficker for services provided by his or her spouse, the court will look sceptically at the arrangement to make sure that the consideration not only is real but is realistically valued. Were this not done, then the object of the Act would be easily defeated."

R. v. *Chapman* (para. 30.05) is concerned with the valuation of a house purchased by a wife partly with money provided by her convicted husband, partly with her own money and partly with a mortgage.

Statements by the prosecution and the defence

30.04 The prosecution must apply to the court for a requirement to be made under section 3(2) so as to bring into operation section 3(3).

Re T. (1993) 96 Cr.App.R. 194, C.A. was concerned with issues of self-incrimination (see para. 31.02 *post*). In the course of his judgment Parker L.J. said:

> "Section 3 of the 1986 Act, however, enabled the crown court to make orders which were or might be akin to disclosure orders. Section 3(1) was very wide and expressly retrospective. Section 3(2) and (3) together enabled the crown court to assume that the defendant had carried on and benefited from drug trafficking.
>
> Section 3(6) was clearly designed to prevent the defendant from refusing to answer an allegation that an asset was received as a payment or reward for drug trafficking on the ground of self-incrimination.
>
> That section, in his Lordship's judgment, revealed a clear parliamentary intention:
>
> First, that a person convicted of a drug trafficking offence, in addition to being punished for that offence, should be, not punished for other offences of a like nature, but deprived of the benefits of all his other drug trafficking.
>
> Second, that his property should, for that purpose only, be assumed to constitute such benefits in the absence of proof to the contrary.
>
> Third, and most important, that self-incrimination should be no ground for failing to comply with a crown court order under section 3."

The trial judge, after hearing the evidence, made a confiscation order which exceeded by £10,000 the amount claimed by the Crown in a section 3 statement. The court held that the power of the sentencer to determine the amount of the confiscation order was not limited to the amount claimed by the Crown: *R. v. Atkinson* [1992] Crim.L.R. 749 followed in *R. v. Finch* [1992] Crim.L.R. 901.

Practice Direction Rules have been made by the Crown Court at Isleworth. They are set out in Appendix XXVII.

Section 3 has been substantially amended by section 10 of the Criminal Justice Act 1993. Section 10 is set out in Appendix XXXVII, *post*. A new section 3A will be inserted by section 10(5). This will enable the court to order the defendant to provide information and to draw inferences from a failure.

Assessing the proceeds

30.05 Where a house is subject to a mortgage, section 5(4) provides that the amount required to discharge the mortgage shall be deducted before arriving at the value. However, the proportion of the original value of the house attributable to the sum raised by mortgage will have increased proportionally as the value of the house increased. If there is more than one owner, or the house is a gift caught by the Act, effect must be given to this concept because these provisions are to be construed as penal.

Where a house had been purchased for £78,000 and registered in the appellant's wife's name, the judge, having heard evidence that £58,000 of the purchase price was the result of the sale of the wife's jewellery, was entitled to reject that evidence and find that the money was attributable to the appellant's drug trafficking. It followed that the money was a gift caught by the Act. To assess the realisable value of the asset resulting from the gift required close analysis of the provisions of section 5. Section 5(5)(*a*) is concerned with changes in the value of money whereas section 5(5)(*b*) is concerned with changes in the value of property. The value of the property had increased more than the change in the value of money and therefore section 5(5)(*b*) applied. There had been a mortgage of £20,000. The judge correctly took the value of the house at the material time as £150,000 and applied the formula 58/78 × 150,000 resulting in his assessing the value of the appellants proceeds as £111,540. This, however, ignored section 5(4)(*a*)(ii). The mortgage redemption figure of £20,353 fell to be deducted from the total value of the house resulting in a formula of 58/78 × 129,646 and in the correct assessment of £96,403: *R.* v. *Chapman* [1991] T.L.R. 518.

Value of drugs

30.05A The appellant had pleaded guilty to possessing 999.14 grams of amphetamine with intent to supply. The judge found that the appellant had not been drug trafficking before and that his sole benefit was the actual drugs found. He valued them at the retail street value, not at the cost of acquiring them wholesale. The Court of Appeal did not criticise the basis of the valuation but held that the drugs could not be a payment or other reward since it was a first time drug trafficking offence: *R.* v. *Butler* (1993) Crim.L.R. 320, C.A.

Assumptions

30.06 Section 2(3)(*a*)(i) and (ii) have been the subject of discussion amongst commentators. The assumptions apply to any property held by the defendant at the date of his conviction regardless of whether he acquired it outside the period beginning with six years before the institution of proceedings: *Re Thomas* (May 26, 1992, C.A., unreported).

The Court of Appeal gave guidance on how a judge should decide whether to make assumptions under section 2(3) in the case of *R.* v.

Redbourne [1992] 1 W.L.R. 1182, C.A. No question of the standard of proof arose when the judge was deciding whether the assumptions should be made. That was essentially a threshold decision, whenever it was made. It was not necessary or sensible to apply any standard or proof to the question whether there was reason to suspect that the defendant had benefited from drug trafficking. If the assumptions were not rebutted, then the court had to, or might, take the assumed facts as true. It mattered not for that purpose whether the standard of proof was criminal or civil. Whichever standard was appropriate, the assumed fact was to be treated as true. Guidance was given to prevent any misunderstanding of passages in the judgment of Lord Lane in *R. v. Dickens.*

The court will be required to make assumptions and to give reasons in the case of any assumption not so applied. (See section 9 of the Criminal Justice Act 1993 set out in Appendix XXXVII.)

Burden of proof

30.07   The decision in *Dickens* was further considered by the Court of Appeal in *R. v. Redbourne* [1992] 1 W.L.R. 1182, C.A., where it was held that:

> "If a court was directed or empowered to make assumptions that meant the court had to or might take the assumed facts as true. It mattered not for that purpose whether the standard of proof was criminal or civil. Whichever standard was appropriate, the assumed fact was still to be treated as true."

If a defendant failed to rebut the assumption on the balance of probabilities, the assumption stood as a fact (see also *ante*, para. 30.06).

The Criminal Justice Act 1993, s.7(2) has amended section 1 by the addition of a new subsection (7A) which specifies that the civil standard of proof shall apply to the questions of whether a person has benefited from drug trafficking or the amount to be recovered. (Set out in Appendix XXXVII, *post.*)

Enforcement as for a fine

30.08   It is logical to sentence the defendant for his offence and then to impose the period to be served in default of payment: *R. v. Chapman, The Times,* November 18, 1991.

Section 13 of the Criminal Justice Act 1993 amends section 6 of the Act to the effect that a prisoner cannot satisfy a confiscation order by serving imprisonment in default of payment.

A sentence in default must be imposed even if the police or Customs hold an appropriate sum of the defendant's money. The Customs do not have power to pay it to the magistrates' court in satisfaction of the order: *R.* v. *Popple and others* [1992] Crim.L.R. 675 (not reported in full on this point); *R.* v. *Valencia-Cardenas,* March 9, 1992, unreported, was *per incuriam.*

The maximum periods of imprisonment in default are set out in the Powers of Criminal Courts Act 1973, s.31 (as amended). Where there has been part-payment the period of imprisonment will be reduced proportionately: section 31(3B).

Definitions

30.09 The appeal of *Colin David Richards* (1992) 95 Cr.App.R. 230 illustrates the effect of slack procedure in the Crown Court. The trial judge failed to certify that he had made an assumption under section 2(3) and gave no reason for his finding that a loan of £6,000 was received "in connection with drug trafficking." The judge considered it irrelevant that the appellant may not have known at the time he received it, that it was "given in connection with drug trafficking." The Court of Appeal held that if the appellant received it believing it to be a loan unconnected with drug trafficking, he did not receive it within the terms of section 1(3).

How it works in practice

30.10 The defendant is entitled to give evidence. The court is entitled to have regard to evidence and exhibits given at the preceding trial without the witnesses being recalled: *R.* v. *Jenkins* [1991] Crim.L.R. 481.

The court must have accurate contemporary information concerning the value of property. Estimating the value of real property is not a precise science and some safety margin for error must be allowed. An up-to-date professional valuation of a house is required: *R.* v. *Lemmon* (1992) 13 Cr.App.R.(S.) 66. (The Court of Appeal did not mention that the appellant could have applied for variation under section 14 (para. 33.01 *post*).)

A husband and wife were charged with conspiracy to supply cocaine. The husband escaped. The appellant was left in control of property in excess of £2 million and a confiscation order was made for £2,676,627. The Court of Appeal was referred to the decision in *Porter* [1990] 1 W.L.R. 1260. It held that where only one defendant had been convicted and that defendant had sufficient control to realise the property, there was no reason why an order to realise the total sum should not be made against her: *R.* v. *Chrastny (No. 2)* (1991) 93 Cr.App.R. 406.

A sentence in default must be imposed even if the police or the Customs hold an appropriate sum of the defendant's money. The Customs do not have power to pay it to the magistrates' court in satisfaction of the order: *R.* v. *Popple and others* [1992] Crim.L.R. 675 (not reported in full on this point); *R.* v. *Valencia-Cardenas*, March 9, 1992, unreported, was *per incuriam.*

Appeal

30.12 Where a judge purported to correct a defective order some two years later relying on *R.* v. *Saville* [1980] Q.B. 12 and, in particular, added a sentence of two years' imprisonment in default, the Court of Appeal held that the variation went beyond the confines of the principles in that case: *R.* v. *Onwuka* (1992) 95 Cr.App.R. 47.

Where the value of the matrimonial home was based on a concession made in court which the appellant now wished to withdraw, his proper course was an application for variation under section 14. (See para. 33.01 of the main work). *R.* v. *Atkinson* [1992] Crim.L.R. 749.

CHAPTER 31

Interim Orders

When interim orders can be made

31.02   Where the High Court makes a restraint order freezing the defendant's assets, it can also order the defendant to swear an affidavit disclosing the full value, nature and whereabouts of all his assets: *Re T.* (1993) 96 Cr.App.R. 194, C.A. Self-incrimination is not a reason for refusing such an order.

CHAPTER 32

Realisation etc. of Assets

Appointment of receiver

32.01 The case of *Re. B.* (May 13, 1991, D.C., unreported (see para. 30.03, *ante*)) is an example of an appliction by a wife under section 11(8) in respect of her interest in a matrimonial home. Since there was no provision for her to be represented at the Crown Court, the finding incorporated in the confiscation order was not binding on her. Having found in her favour in respect of a proportion of her claim, Henry J. ordered that her costs should be paid out of the funds realised by the receiver.

Scotland

32.05 Drug Trafficking Offences (Enforcement in England and Wales) Order 1988 (S.I. 1988 No. 593) deals with enforcement of Scottish orders in England and Wales.

Northern Ireland and external orders

32.06 Criminal Justice (International Co-operation) Act 1990 (Enforcement of Overseas Forfeiture Orders) (Northern Ireland) Order 1991 (S.I. 1991 No. 1464) deals with enforcement of Northern Ireland orders in England and Wales.

Great Britain has confiscation agreements with the following countries:

April 11, 1989 : U.S.A.
June 21, 1990 : Switzerland
August 4, 1990 : Canada
September 12, 1990 : Australia
September 23, 1990 : Gibraltar
October 1, 1990 : Mexico
October 24, 1990 : Bahamas
December 15, 1990 : Spain
August 28, 1991 : Cayman Islands, Hong Kong

September 20, 1991: Saudi Arabia
April 1, 1992: Sweden

Being negotiated:

Anguilla   India
Argentina   Italy
Bahrain   Malaysia
Barbados   Montserrat
Bermuda   Nigeria
Ecuador   South Africa
Germany   Uruguay
Guyana

CHAPTER 33

Variation and Compensation

Variation of confiscation orders

33.01   A section 5A has been inserted by section 12 of the Criminal Justice Act 1993 (set out in Schedule XXXVII *post*) enabling the prosecution to apply to the Crown Court, within six years of a determination, for an increase in the value of benefit.

CHAPTER 35

Offences and Disclosure

Defences

35.02 The Court of Appeal in *R.* v. *Colle* (1991) 135 S.J. (LB) 125 confirmed that defences under subsection (4) have to be established on the balance of probabilities. The prosecution do not have to disprove them.

Concealing or transferring proceeds of drug trafficking

35.06 Sections 16 and 17 of the Criminal Justice Act 1993 will amend the DTOA 1986 by the addition of a new section 23A (set out in Appendix XXXVII together with a new section 42A to be added to the Criminal Justice (Scotland) Act 1987). This creates a new offence of knowingly acquiring property which represents another person's proceeds of drug trafficking.

Sections 18 and 19 will amend the DTOA 1986 by the addition of new sections 26B and 26C together with new sections 43A and 43B to be added to the Criminal Justice (Scotland) Act 1987. These create new and drastic offences of failing to disclose knowledge or *suspicion* of laundering drug money and a new offence of tipping-off a suspect concerning an investigation into laundering drug money.

Section 20 will add a new section 36A empowering the Customs and Excise to institute proceedings for offences under sections 23A, 24, 26B, 26C or 31 and section 14 of the Criminal Justice (International Co-operation) Act 1990.

The Postal Packets (Customs and Excise) (Amendment) Regulations 1992

(S.I. No. 3224)

Made	*16th December 1992*
Coming in force	*1st January 1993*

The Treasury, by virtue of the powers conferred on them by section 16(2) of the Post Office Act 1953, and all other powers enabling them in that behalf, and on the recommendation of the Commissioners of Customs and Excise and, after consultation with the Post Office, of the Secretary of State, hereby make the following Regulations:

1. These Regulations may be cited as the Postal Packets (Customs and Excise) (Amendment) Regulations 1992 and shall come into force on 1st January 1993.
2. In these Regulations—
"Community goods" shall have the meaning given by Article 1.2(e) of Council Regulation (EEC) No. 4151/88;
"territory of the Community" shall have the meaning given by Article 3.1 of Council Directive 77/388/EEC.
3. The Postal Packets (Customs and Excise) Regulations 1986 shall be amended as follows—
(a) Regulation 5(b) shall be omitted;
(b) after Regulation 5 there shall be inserted the following—
"**5A.** In its application to goods contained in postal packets brought into the United Kingdom, Regulation 5 of the Customs Controls on Importation of Goods Regulations 1991 shall apply only in any case, or class of cases, in which the Commissioners require an entry to be made in accordance with that Regulation.";
(c) for Regulation 9(2), there shall be substituted the following—
"(2) Regulations 7 and 8 of these regulations and paragraph (1) of this Regulation shall not apply to a postal packet or mail bag which—
(a) contains only Community goods, and
(i) having been posted elsewhere in the territory of the Community, is brought by post to the United Kingdom for delivery there, or
(ii) is posted in the United Kingdom for delivery elsewhere in the territory of the Community; or
(b) is posted in a place situated outside the United Kingdom for delivery in another place so situated."

Criminal Justice (International Co-operation) Act 1990

(CHAPTER 5)

Section 7

Officers of the Customs and Excise may exercise the powers of a constable. See the Criminal Justice (International Co-operation) Act 1990 (Exercise of Powers) Order 1991 (S.I. 1991 No. 1297) set out in Appendix XXX *post.*

Section 25

The prescribed sum is £10,000: Criminal Justice (International Co-operation) Act 1990 (Detention and Forfeiture of Drug Trafficking Cash) Order 1991 (S.I. 1991 No. 1816).

Section 26

See rules 9-12 of the Magistrates' Courts Rules 1991: Magistrates' Courts (Detention and Forfeiture of Drug Trafficking Cash) Rules 1991 (S.I. 1991 No. 1923) set out in Appendix XXXIII *post.*

Schedule 2

The following drugs are added by virtue of the Criminal Justice (International Co-operation) Act 1990 (Modification) Order 1992 (S.I. 1992 No. 2873) with effect from January 1, 1993.

TABLE 1

N-Acetylanthranilic Acid
Isosafrole
3,4-Methylenedioxy-
phenyl-2-propanone
Piperonal
Safrole

TABLE 2

Hydrochloric Acid
Methyl Ethyl Ketone
Potassium Permanganate
Sulphuric Acid
Toluene

Single Convention on Narcotic Drugs 1961

(As amended by the 1972 Protocol amending the Single Convention on Narcotic Drugs, 1961)

Revised Schedules including all amendments made by the Commission on Narcotic Drugs in force as of 5 March 1990

Amendment

Replace the Schedules by the following text.

SCHEDULES

List of Drugs included in Schedule I

ACETORPHINE (3-*O*-acetyltetrahydro-7α-(1-hydroxy-1-methylbutyl)-6,14-*endo*etheno-oripavine)
ACETYL-ALPHA-METHYLFENTANYL (*N*-[1-(α-methylphenethyl)-4-piperidyl]acetanilide)
ACETYLMETHADOL (3-acetoxy-6-dimethylamino-4,4-diphenylheptane)
ALFENTANIL (*N*-[1-[2-(4-ethyl-4,5-dihydro-5-oxo-1*H*-tetrazol-1-yl)ethyl]-4-(methoxymethyl)-4-piperidinyl]-*N*-phenylpropanamide)
ALLYLPRODINE (3-allyl-1-methyl-4-phenyl-4-propionoxypiperidine)
ALPHACETYLMETHADOL (*alpha*-3-acetoxy-6-dimethylamino-4,4-diphenylheptane)
ALPHAMEPRODINE (*alpha*-3-ethyl-1-methyl-4-phenyl-4-propionoxypiperidine)
ALPHAMETHADOL (*alpha*-6-dimethylamino-4,4-diphenyl-3-heptanol)
ALPHA-METHYLFENTANYL (*N*-[1-(α-methylphenethyl)-4-piperidyl]propionanilide)
ALPHA-METHYLTHIOFENTANYL (*N*-[1-methyl-2-(2-thienyl)ethyl]-4-piperidyl] propionanilide)
ALPHAPRODINE (alpha-1,3-dimethyl-4-phenyl-4-propionoxypiperidine)
ANILERIDINE (1-*para*-aminophenethyl-4-phenylpiperidine-4-carboxylic acid ethyl ester)

BENZETHIDINE (1-(2-benzyloxyethyl)-4-phenylpiperidine-4-carboxylic acid
ethyl ester)
BENZYLMORPHINE (3-benzylmorphine)
BETACETYLMETHADOL (*beta*-3-acetoxy-6-dimethylamino-4,4-
diphenylheptane)
BETA-HYDROXYFENTANYL (*N*-[1-(β-hydroxyphenethyl)-4-
piperidyl]propionanilide)
BETA-HYDROXY-3-METHYLFENTANYL (*N*-[1-(β-hydroxyphenethyl)-3-
methyl-4-piperidyl]propionanilide)
BETAMEPRODINE (*beta*-3-ethyl-1-methyl-4-phenyl-4-propionoxypiperidine)
BETAMETHADOL (*beta*-6-dimethylamino-4,4-diphenyl-3-heptanol)
BETAPRODINE (*beta*-1,3-dimethyl-4-phenyl-4-propionoxypiperidine)
BEZITRAMIDE (1-(3-cyano-3,3-diphenylpropyl)-4-(2-oxo-3-propionyl-
1-benzimidazolinyl)-piperidine)
CANNABIS and CANNABIS RESIN and EXTRACTS and TINCTURES
OF CANNABIS
CLONITAZENE (2-*para*-chlorbenzyl-1-diethylaminoethyl-5-
nitrobenzimidazole)
COCA LEAF
COCAINE (methyl ester of benzoylecgonine)
CODOXIME (dihydrocodeinone-6-carboxymethyloxime)
CONCENTRATE OF POPPY STRAW (the material arising when poppy
straw has entered into a process for the concentration of its alkaloids when
such material is made available in trade)
DESOMORPHINE (dihydrodeoxymorphine)
DEXTROMORAMIDE ((+)-4-[2-methyl-4-oxo-3,3-diphenyl-4-(1-
pyrrolidinyl)butyl] morpholine)
DIAMPROMIDE (*N*-[2-(methylphenethylamino)propyl]propionanilide)
DIETHYLTHIAMBUTENE (3-diethylamino-1,1-di-(2'-thienyl)-1-butene)
DIFENOXIN (1-(3-cyano-3,3-diphenylpropyl)-4-phenylisonipecotic acid)
DIHYDROMORPHINE
DIMENOXADOL (2-dimethylaminoethyl-1-ethoxy-1,1-diphenylacetate)
DIMEPHEPTANOL (6-dimethylamino-4,4-diphenyl-3-heptanol)
DIMETHYLTHIAMBUTENE (3-dimethylamino-1,1-di-(2'-thienyl)-1-butene)
DIOXAPHETYL BUTYRATE (ethyl-4-morpholino-2,2-diphenylbutyrate)
DIPHENOXYLATE (1-(3-cyano-3,3-diphenylpropyl)-4-phenylpiperidine-4-
carboxylic acid ethyl ester)
DIPIPANONE (4,4-diphenyl-6-piperidine-3-heptanone)
DROTEBANOL (3,4-dimethoxy-17-methylmorphinan-6β,14-diol)
ECGONINE, its esters and derivatives which are convertible to ecgonine and
cocaine
ETHYLMETHYLTHIAMBUTENE (3-ethylmethylamino-1,1-di-(2'-
thienyl)-1-butene)
ETONITAZENE (1-diethylaminoethyl-2-*para*-ethoxybenzyl-5-
nitrobenzimidazole)
ETORPHINE (tetrahydro-7α-(1-hydroxy-1-methylbutyl)-
6,14-*endo*etheno-oripavine)
ETOXERIDINE (1-[2-(2-hydroxyethoxy)-ethyl]-4-phenylpiperidine-4-
carboxylic acid ethyl ester)
FENTANYL (1-phenethyl-4-*N*-propionylanilinopiperidine)

FURETHIDINE (1-(2-tetrahydrofurfuryloxyethyl)-4-phenylpiperidine-4-carboxylic acid ethyl ester)
HEROIN (diacetylmorphine)
HYDROCODONE (dihydrocodeinone)
HYDROMORPHINOL (14-hydroxydihydromorphine)
HYDROMORPHONE (dihydromorphinone)
HYDROXYPETHIDINE (4-*meta*-hydroxyphenyl-1-methylpiperidine-4-carboxylic acid ethyl ester)
ISOMETHADONE (6-dimethylamino-5-methyl-4,4-diphenyl-3-hexanone)
KETOBEMIDONE (4-*meta*-hydroxyphenyl-1-methyl-4-propionylpiperidine)
LEVOMETHORPHAN* ((-)-3-methoxy-*N*-methylmorphinan)
LEVOMORAMIDE ((-)-4-[2-methyl-4-oxo-3,3-diphenyl-4-(1-pyrrolidinyl)butyl]morpholine)
LEVOPHENACYLMORPHAN ((-)-3-hydroxy-*N*-phenacylmorphinan)
LEVORPHANOL* ((-)-3-hydroxy-*N*-methylmorphinan)
METAZOCINE (2'-hydroxy-2,5,9-trimethyl-6,7-benzomorphan)
METHADONE (6-dimethylamino-4,4-diphenyl-3-heptanone)
METHODONE INTERMEDIATE (4-cyano-2-dimethylamino-4,4-diphenylbutane)
METHYLDESORPHINE (6-methyl-*delta*-6-deoxymorphine)
METHYLDIHYDROMORPHINE (6-methyldihydromorphine)
3-METHYLFENTANYL (*N*-(3-methyl-1-phenethyl-4-piperidyl) propionanilide); (*cis*-*N*-[3-methyl-1-(2-phenylethyl)-4-piperidyl]propionanilide); (*trans*-*N*-[3-methyl-1-(2-phenylethyl)-4-piperidyl]propionanilide)
3-METHYLTHIOFENTANYL (*N*-[3-methyl-1-[2-(2-thienyl)ethyl]-4-piperidyl]propionanilide)
METOPON (5-methyldihydromorphinone)
MORAMIDE INTERMEDIATE (2-methyl-3-morpholino-1,1-diphenylpropane carboxylic acid)
MORPHERIDINE (1-(2-morpholinoethyl)-4-phenylpiperidine-4-carboxylic acid ethyl ester)
MORPHINE
MORPHINE METHOBROMIDE and other pentavalent nitrogen morphine derivatives
MORPHINE-N-OXIDE
MPPP (1-methyl-4-phenyl-4-piperidinol propionate (ester))
MYROPHINE (myristylbenzylmorphine)
NICOMORPHINE (3,6-dinicotinylmorphine)
NORACYMETHADOL ((±)-*alpha*-3-acetoxy-6-methylamino-4,4-diphenylheptane)
NORLEVORPHANOL ((-)-3-hydroxymorphinan)
NORMETHADONE (6-dimethylamino-4,4-diphenyl-3-hexanone)
NORMORPHINE (demethylmorphine)
NORPIPANONE (4,4-diphenyl-6-piperidino-3-hexanone)
OPIUM
OXYCODONE (14-hydroxydihydrocodeinone)
OXYMORPHONE (14-hydroxydihydromorphinone)

---

* Dextromethorphan ((+)-3-methoxy-N-methylmorphinan) and dextrorphan ((+)-3-hydroxy-N-methyl-morphinan) are specifically excluded from this Schedule.

PARA-FLUOROFENTANYL (4'-fluoro-*N*-(1-phenethyl-4-piperidyl) propionanilide)
PEPAP (1-phenethyl-4-phenyl-4-piperidinol acetate (ester))
PETHIDINE (1-methyl-4-phenylpiperidine-4-carboxylic acid ethyl ester)
PETHIDINE INTERMEDIATE A (4-cyano-1-methyl-4-phenylpiperidine)
PETHIDINE INTERMEDIATE B (4-phenylpiperidine-4-carboxylic acid ethyl ester)
PETHIDINE INTERMEDIATE C (1-methyl-4-phenylpiperidine-4-carboxylic acid)
PHENADOXONE (6-morpholino-4,4-diphenyl-3-heptanone)
PHENAMPROMIDE (*N*-(1-methyl-2-piperidinoethyl)propionanilide)
PHENAZOCINE (2'-hydroxy-5,9-dimethyl-2-phenethyl-6,7-benzomorphan)
PHENOMORPHAN (3-hydroxy-*N*-phenethylmorphinan)
PHENOPERIDINE (1-(3-hydroxy-3-phenylpropyl)-4-phenylpiperidine-4-carboxylic acid ethyl ester)
PIMINODINE (4-phenyl-1-(3-phenylaminopropyl)piperidine-4-carboxylic acid ethyl ester)
PIRITRAMIDE (1-(3-cyano-3,3-diphenylpropyl)-4-(1-piperidino)piperidine-4-carboxylic acid amide)
PROHEPTAZINE (1,3-dimethyl-4-phenyl-4-propionoxyazacycloheptane)
PROPERIDINE (1-methyl-4-phenylpiperidine-4-carboxylic acid isopropyl ester)
RACEMETHORPHAN ((±)-3-methoxy-*N*-methylmorphinan)
RACEMORAMIDE ((±)-4-[2-methyl-4-oxo-3,3-diphenyl-4-(1-pyrrolidinyl)butyl]morpholine)
RACEMORPHAN ((±)-3-hydroxy-*N*-methylmorphinan)
SUFENTANIL (*N*-[4-(methoxymethyl)-1-[2-(2-thienyl)ethyl]-4-piperidyl]propionanilide)
THEBACON (acetyldihydrocodeinone)
THEBAINE
THIOFENTANYL (*N*-[1-[2-(2-thienyl)ethyl]-4-piperidyl]propionanilide)
TILIDINE ((±)-ethyl *trans*-2-(dimethylamino)-1-phenyl-3-cyclohexene-1-carboxylate)
TRIMEPERIDINE (1,2,5-trimethyl-4-phenyl-4-propionoxypiperidine); and

The isomers, unless specifically excepted, of the drugs in this Schedule whenever the existence of such isomers is possible within the specific chemical designation;

The esters and ethers, unless appearing in another Schedule, of the drugs in this Schedule whenever the existence of such esters or ethers is possible;

The salts of the drugs listed in this Schedule, including the salts of esters, ethers and isomers as provided above whenever the existence of such salts is possible.

List of Drugs included in Schedule II

ACETYLDIHYDROCODEINE
CODEINE (3-methylmorphine)
DEXTROPROPOXYPHENE (α-(+)-4-dimethylamino-1,2-diphenyl-3-methyl-2-butanol propionate)
DIHYDROCODEINE

ETHYLMORPHINE (3-ethylmorphine)
NICOCODINE (6-nicotinylcodeine)
NICODICODINE (6-nicotinyldihydrocodeine)
NORCODEINE (*N*-demethylcodeine)
PHOLCODINE (morpholinylethylmorphine)
PROPIRAM (*N*-(1-methyl-2-piperidinoethyl)-*N*-2-pyridylpropionamide); and

The isomers, unless specifically excepted, of the drugs in this Schedule whenever the existence of such isomers is possible within the specific chemical designation;
The salts of the drugs listed in this Schedule, including the salts of the isomers as provided above whenever the existence of such salts is possible.

List of Preparations included in Schedule III

1. Preparations of Acetyldihydrocodeine,
               Codeine,
               Dihydrocodeine,
               Ethylmorphine,
               Nicocodine,
               Nicodicodine,
               Norcodeine, and
               Pholcodine

when compounded with one or more other ingredients and containing not more than 100 milligrams of the drug per dosage unit and with a concentration of not more than 2.5 per cent in undivided preparations.

2. Preparations of propiram containing not more than 100 milligrams of propiram per dosage unit and compounded with at least the same amount of methylcellulose.

3. Preparations of dextropropoxyphene for oral use containing not more than 135 milligrams of dextropropoxyphene base per dosage unit or with a concentration of not more than 2.5 per cent in undivided preparations, provided that such preparations do not contain any substance controlled under the 1971 Convention on Psychotropic Substances.

4. Preparations of cocaine containing not more than 0.1 per cent of cocaine calculated as cocaine base and preparations of opium or morphine containing not more than 0.2 per cent of morphine calculated as anhydrous morphine base and compounded with one or more other ingredients and in such a way that the drug cannot be recovered by readily applicable means or in a yield which would constitute a risk to public health.

5. Preparations of difenoxin containing, per dosage unit, not more than 0.5 milligram of difenoxin and a quantity of atropine sulphate equivalent to at least 5 per cent of the dose of difenoxin.

6. Preparations of diphenoxylate containing, per dosage unit, not more than 2.5 milligrams of diphenoxylate calculated as base and a quantity of atropine sulphate equivalent to at least one per cent of the dose of diphenoxylate.

7. *Pulvis ipecacuanhae et opii compositus*

10 per cent opium in powder,
10 per cent Ipecacuanha root, in powder
well mixed with
80 per cent of any other powdered ingredient containing no drug.

8. Preparations conforming to any of the formulae listed in this Schedule and mixtures of such preparations with any material which contains no drug.

List of Drugs included in Schedule IV

ACETORPHINE (3-*O*-acetyltetrahydro-7α-(1-hydroxy-1-methylbutyl)-6,14-*endo*etheno-oripavine)
ACETYL-ALPHA-METHYLFENTANYL (*N*-[1-(α-methylphenethyl)-4-piperidyl]acetanilide)
ALPHA-METHYLFENTANYL (*N*-[1-(α-methylphenethyl)-4-piperidyl]propionanilide)
ALPHA-METHYLTHIOFENTANYL (*N*-[1-[1-methyl-2-(2-thienyl)ethyl]-4-piperidyl] propionanilide)
BETA-HYDROXYFENTANYL (*N*-[1-(β-hydroxyphenethyl)-4-piperidyl]propionanilide)
BETA-HYDROXY-3-METHYLFENTANYL (*N*-[1-(β-hydroxyphenethyl)-3-methyl-4-piperidyl]propionanilide)
CANNABIS and CANNABIS RESIN
DESOMORPHINE (dihydrodeoxymorphine)
ETORPHINE (tetrahydro-7α-(1-hydroxy-1-methylbutyl)-6,14-*endo*etheno-oripavine)
HEROIN (diacetylmorphine)
KETOBEMIDONE (4-*meta*-hydroxyphenyl-1-methyl-4-propionylpiperidine)
3-METHYLFENTANYL (*N*-(3-methyl-1-phenethyl-4-piperidyl) propionanilide); (*cis-N*-[3-methyl-1-(2-phenylethyl)-4-piperidyl]propionanilide); (*trans-N*-[3-methyl-1-(2-phenylethyl)-4-piperidyl]propionanilide)
3-METHYLTHIOFENTANYL (*N*-[3-methyl-1-[2-(2-thienyl)ethyl]-4-piperidyl]propionanilide)
MPPP (1-methyl-4-phenyl-4-piperidinol propionate (ester))
PARA-FLUOROFENTANYL (4'-fluoro-*N*-(1-phenethyl-4-piperidyl)propionanilide)
PEPAP (1-phenethyl-4-phenyl-4-piperidinol acetate (ester))
THIOFENTANYL (*N*-[1-[2-(2-thienyl)ethyl]-4-piperidyl]propionanilide); and

The salts of the drugs listed in this Schedule whenever the formation of such salts is possible.

Convention on Psychotropic Substances 1971

**Revised Schedules including all amendments made by the
Commission on Narcotic Drugs in force as of 7 December 1991**

Amendment

Replace the Schedules by the following text.

LIST OF SUBSTANCES IN THE SCHEDULES

List of Substances in Schedule I

	International nonproprietary name	*Other nonproprietary or trivial names*	*Chemical name*
1.	BROLAMFETAMINE	DOB	(±)-4-bromo-2,5-dimethoxy-α-methylphenethylamine
2.	CATHINONE		(−)-(*S*)-2-aminopropiophenone
3.		DET	3-[2-(diethylamino)ethyl]indole
4.		DMA	(±)-2,5-dimethoxy-α-methyl-phenethylamine
5.		DMHP	3-(1,2-dimethylheptyl)-7,8,9,10-tetrahydro-6,6,9-trimethyl-6*H*-dibenzo[*b,d*]pyran-1-ol
6.		DMT	3-[2-(dimethylamino)ethyl]indole
7.		DOET	(±)-4-ethyl-2,5-dimethoxy-α-phenethylamine
8.	*N*-ETHYL-TENAMFETAMINE	MDE, *N*-ETHYL-MDA	(±)-*N*-ethyl-α-methyl-3,4-(methylenedioxy)phenethylamine
9.	ETICYCLIDINE	PCE	*N*-ethyl-1-phenylcyclohexylamine
10.	*N*-HYDROXY-TENAMFET-AMINE	*N*-OH MDA, *N*-HYDROXY-MDA	(±)-*N*-[α-methyl-3,4-(methylene-dioxy)phenethyl]hydroxyl-amine
11.	(+)-LYSERGIDE	LSD, LSD-25	9,10-didehydro-*N,N*-diethyl-6-methylergoline-8β-carboxamide
12.		MDMA	(±)-*N*,α-dimethyl-3,4-(methylene-dioxy)phenethylamine
13.		mescaline	3,4,5-trimethoxyphenethylamine
14.	4-METHYLAMINO-REX		(±)-*cis*-2-amino-4-methyl-5-phenyl-2-oxazoline (±)-*cis*-4,5-dihydro-4-methyl-5-phenyl-2-oxazolamine

International nonproprietary name	Other nonproprietary or trivial names	Chemical name
15.	MMDA	2-methoxy-α-methyl-4,5-(methylenedioxy)phenethylamine
16.	parahexyl	3-hexyl-7,8,9,10-tetrahydro-6,6,9-trimethyl-6*H*-dibenzo[*b,d*] pyran-1-ol
17.	PMA	*p*-methoxy-α-methylphen-ethylamine
18.	psilocine, psilotsin	3-[2-(dimethylamino)ethyl] indol-4-ol
19. PSILOCYBINE		3-[2-(dimethylamino)ethyl]indol-4-yl dihydrogen phosphate
20. ROLICYCLIDINE	PHP, PCPY	1-(1-phenylcyclohexyl)pyrrolidine
21.	STP, DOM	2,5-dimethoxy-α,4-dimethyl-phenethylamine
22. TENAMFETAMINE	MDA	α-methyl-3,4-(methylenedioxy) phenethylamine
23. TENOCYCLIDINE	TCP	1-[1-(2-thienyl)cyclohexyl]piperidine
24.	tetrahydrocannabinol, the following isomers and their stereochemical variants	
		7,8,9,10-tetrahydro-6,6,9-trimethyl-3-pentyl-6*H*-dibenzo[*b,d*] pyran-1-ol
		(9*R*, 10*aR*)-8,9,10,10*a*-tetrahydro-6,6,9-trimethyl-3-pentyl-6*H*-dibenzo[*b,d*]pyran-1-ol
		(6*aR*, 9*R*, 10*aR*)-6*a*,9,10,10*a*-tetrahydro-6,6,9-trimethyl-3-pentyl-6*H*-dibenzo[*b,d*]pyran-1-ol
		(6*aR*, 10*aR*)-6*a*,7,10,10*a*-tetrahydro 6,6,9-trimethyl-3-pentyl-6*H*-dibenzo[*b,d*]pyran-1-ol
		6*a*,7,8,9-tetrahydro-6,6,9-trimethyl-3-pentyl-6*H*-dibenzo[*b,d*] pyran-1-ol
		(6*aR*, 10*aR*)-6*a*,7,8,9,10,10*a*-hexa-hydro-6,6-dimethyl-9-methylene-3-pentyl-6*H*-dibenzo[*b,d*] pyran-1-ol
25.	TMA	(±)-3,4,5-trimethoxy-α-methylphen-ethylamine

The salts of the substances listed in this Schedule whenever the existence of such salts is possible.

List of Substances in Schedule II

International nonproprietary name	Other nonproprietary or trivial names	Chemical name
1. AMFETAMINE	amphetamine	(±)-α-methylphenethylamine
2. DEXAMFETAMINE	dexamphetamine	(+)-α-methylphenethylamine
3. DRONABINOL	(−)-*trans*-Δ-9-tetrahydro-cannabinol	(6*aR*, 10*aR*)-6*a*,7,8,10*a*-tetrahydro-6,6,9-trimethyl-3-pentyl-6*H*-dibenzo[*b,d*]pyran-1-ol
4. FENETYLLINE		7-[2-[α-methylphenethyl)amino] ethyl]theophylline
5. LEVAMFETAMINE	levamphetamine levomethamphetamine	(−)-(*R*)-α-methylphenethylamine (−)-*N*,α-dimethylphenethylamine
7. MECLOQUALONE		3-(*o*-chlorophenyl)-2-methyl-4(3*H*)-quinazolinone

International nonproprietary name	*Other nonproprietary or trivial names*	*Chemical name*
8. METAMFETAMINE	methamphetamine	(+)-(*S*)-*N*-α-dimethylphenethylamine
9. METAMFETAMINE RACEMATE	methamphetamine racemate	(±)-*N*,α-dimethylphenethylamine
10. METHAQUALONE		2-methyl-3-*o*-tolyl-4(3*H*)-quinazolinone
11. METHYLPHENIDATE		Methyl α-phenyl-2-piperidineacetate
12. PHENCYCLIDINE	PCP	1-(1-phenylcyclohexyl)piperidine
13. PHENMETRAZINE		3-methyl-2-phenylmorpholine
14. SECOBARBITAL		5-allyl-5-(1-methylbutyl)barbituric acid

The salts of the substances listed in this Schedule whenever the existence of such salts is possible.

List of Substances in Schedule III

International nonproprietary name	*Other nonproprietary or trivial names*	*Chemical name*
1. AMOBARBITAL		5-ethyl-5-isopentylbarbituric acid
2. BUPRENORPHINE		21-cyclopropyl-7-α-[(*S*)-1-hydroxy-1,2,2-trimethylpropyl]-6,14-*endo*-ethano-6,7,8,14-tetrahydro-oripavine
3. BUTALBITAL		5-allyl-5-isobutylbarbituric acid
4. CATHINE	(+)-norpseudo-ephedrine	(+)-(*R*)-α-[(*R*)-1-aminoethyl]benzyl alcohol
5. CYCLOBARBITAL		5-(1-cyclohexen-1-yl)-5-ethylbarbituric acid
6. GLUTETHIMIDE		2-ethyl-2-phenylglutarimide
7. PENTAZOCINE		(2*R**, 6*R**, 11*R**)-1,2,3,4,5,6-hexahydro-6,11-dimethyl-3-(3-methyl-2-butenyl)-2,6-methano-3-benzazocin-8-ol
8. PENTOBARBITAL		5-ethyl-5-(1-methylbutyl)barbituric acid

The salts of the substances listed in this Schedule whenever the existence of such salts is possible.

List of Substances in Schedule IV

International nonproprietary name	*Other nonproprietary or trivial names*	*Chemical name*
1. ALLOBARBITAL		5,5-diallylbarbituric acid
2. ALPRAZOLAM		8-chloro-1-methyl-6-phenyl-4*H-s*-triazolo[4,3-*a*][1,4]benzodiazepine
3. AMFEPRAMONE		2-(diethylamino)propiophenone
4. BARBITAL		5,5-diethylbarbituric acid
5. BENZFETAMINE	benzphetamine	*N*-benzyl-*N*,α-dimethyl-phenethylamine
6. BROMAZEPAM		7-bromo-1,3-dihydro-5-(2-pyridyl)-2*H*-1,4-benzodiazepin-2-one
7. BUTOBARBITAL		5-butyl-5-ethylbarbituric acid
8. CAMAZEPAM		7-chloro-1,3-dihydro-3-hydroxy-1-methyl-5-phenyl-2*H*-1,4-benzo-diazepin-2-one dimethyl-carbamate (ester)
9. CHLORDIAZEPOXIDE		7-chloro-2-(methylamino)-5-phenyl-3*H*-1,4-benzodiazepine-4-oxide
10. CLOBAZAM		7-chloro-1-methyl-5-phenyl-1*H*-1,5-benzodiazepine-2,4(3*H*,5*H*)-dione
11. CLONAZEPAM		5-(*o*-chlorophenyl)-1,3-dihydro-7-nitro-2*H*-1,4-benzodiazepin-2-one

International nonproprietary name	*Other nonproprietary or trivial names*	*Chemical name*
12. CLORAZEPATE		7-chloro-2,3-dihydro-2-oxo-5-phenyl-1*H*-1,4-benzodiazepine-3-carboxylic acid
13. CLOTIAZEPAM		5-(*o*-chlorophenyl)-7-ethyl-1,3-dihydro-1-methyl-2*H*-thieno [2,3-*e*]-1,4-diazepin-2-one
14. CLOXAZOLAM		10-chloro-11*b*-(*o*-chlorophenyl)-2,3,7,11*b*-tetrahydrooxazolo [3,2-*d*][1,4]benzodiazepin-6(5*H*)-one
15. DELORAZEPAM		7-chloro-5-(*o*-chlorophenyl)-1,3-dihydro-2*H*-1,4-benzodiazepin-2-one
16. DIAZEPAM		7-chloro-1,3-dihydro-1-methyl-5-phenyl-2*H*-1,4-benzodiazepin-2-one
17. ESTAZOLAM		8-chloro-6-phenyl-4*H*-*s*-triazolo [4,3-*a*][1,4]benzodiazepine
18. ETHCHLORVYNOL		1-chloro-3-ethyl-1-penten-4-yn-3-ol
19. ETHINAMATE		1-ethynylcyclohexanol carbamate
20. ETHYL LOFLAZEPATE		Ethyl 7-chloro-5-(*o*-fluorophenyl)-2,3-dihydro-2-oxo-1*H*-1,4-benzodiazepine-3-carboxylate
21. ETILAMFETAMINE	*N*-ethylamphetamine	*N*-ethyl-α-methylphenethylamine
22. FENCAMFAMIN		*N*-ethyl-3-phenyl-2-norbornanamine
23. FENPROPOREX		(±)-3-[(α-methylphenethyl)amino] propionitrile
24. FLUDIAZEPAM		7-chloro-5-(*o*-fluorophenyl)-1,3,-dihydro-1-methyl-2*H*-1,4-benzodiazepin-2-one
25. FLUNITRAZEPAM		5-(*o*-flurophenyl)-1,3-dihydro-1-methyl-7-nitro-2*H*-1,4-benzodiazepin-2-one
26. FLURAZEPAM		7-chloro-1-[2-(diethylamino)ethyl]-5-(*o*-fluorophenyl)-1,3-dihydro-2*H*-1,4-benzodiazepin-2-one
27. HALAZEPAM		7-chloro-1,3-dihydro-5-phenyl-1-(2,2,2-trifluoroethyl)-2*H*-1,4-benzodiazepin-2-one
28. HALOXAZOLAM		10-bromo-11*b*-(*o*-fluorophenyl)-2,3,7,11*b*-tetrahydrooxazolo[3,2-*d*] [1,4]benzodiazepin-6(5*H*)-one
29. KETAZOLAM		11-chloro-8,12*b*-dihydro-2,8-dimethyl-12*b*-phenyl-4*H*-[1,3] oxazino[3,2-*d*][1,4]benzo-diazepine-4,7(6*H*)-dione
30. LEFETAMINE	SPA	(−)-*N*, *N*-dimethyl-1,2-diphenyl-ethylamine
31. LOPRAZOLAM		6-(*o*-chlorophenyl)-2,4-dihydro-2-[(4-methyl-1-piperazinyl) methylene]-8-nitro-1*H*-imidazo [1,2-*a*][1,4]benzodiazepin-1-one
32. LORAZEPAM		7-chloro-5-(*o*-chlorophenyl)-1,3-dihydro-3-hydroxy-2*H*,1,4-benzodiazepin-2-one
33. LORMETAZEPAM		7-chloro-5-(*o*-chlorophenyl)-1,3-dihydro-3-hydroxy-1-methyl-2*H*-1,4-benzodiazepin-2-one
34. MAZINDOL		5-(*p*-chlorophenyl)-2,5-dihydro-3*H*-imidazo[2,1-*a*]isoindol-5-ol
35. MEDAZEPAM		7-chloro-2,3-dihydro-1-methyl-5-phenyl-1*H*-1,4-benzodiazepine

International nonproprietary name	Other nonproprietary or trivial names	Chemical name
36. MEFENOREX		*N*-(3-chloropropyl)-α-methyl-phenethylamine
37. MEPROBAMATE		2-methyl-2-propyl-1,3-propanediol dicarbamate
38. METHYL-PHENOBARBITAL		5-ethyl-1-methyl-5-phenylbarbituric acid
39. METHYPRYLON		3,3-diethyl-5-methyl-2,4-piperidine-dione
40. MIDAZOLAM		8-chloro-6-(*o*-fluorophenyl)-1-methyl-4*H*-imidazo[1,5-*a*][1,4]benzodiazepine
41. NIMETAZEPAM		1,3-dihydro-1-methyl-7-nitro-5-phenyl-2*H*-1,4-benzodiazepin-2-one
42. NITRAZEPAM		1,3-dihydro-7-nitro-5-phenyl-2*H*-1,4-benzodiazepin-2-one
43. NORDAZEPAM		7,chloro-1,3-dihydro-5-phenyl-2*H*-1,4-benzodiazepin-2-one
44. OXAZEPAM		7-chloro-1,3-dihydro-3-hydroxy-5-phenyl-2*H*-1,4-benzodiazepin-2-one
45. OXAZOLAM		10-chloro-2,3,7,11*b*-tetrahydro-2-methyl-11*b*-phenyloxazolo[3,2-*d*)[1,4]benzodiazepin-6(5*H*)-one
46. PEMOLINE		2-amino-5-phenyl-2-oxazolin-4-one 2-imino-5-phenyl-4-oxazolidinone
47. PHENDIMETRAZINE		(+)-(2*S*,3*S*)-3,4-dimethyl-2-phenylmorpholine
48. PHENOBARBITAL		5-ethyl-5-phenylbarbituric acid
49. PHENTERMINE		α,α-dimethylphenethylamine
50. PINAZEPAM		7-chloro-1,3-dihydro-5-phenyl-1-(2-propynyl)-2*H*-1,4-benzo-diazepin-2-one
51. PIPRADROL		α,α-diphenyl-2-piperidinemethanol
52. PRAZEPAM		7-chloro-1-(cyclopropylmethyl)-1,3-dihydro-5-phenyl-2*H*-1,4-benzodiazepin-2-one
53. PYROVALERONE		4′-methyl-2-(1-pyrrolidinyl)valerophenone
54. SECBUTABARBITAL		5-*sec*-butyl-5-ethylbarbituric acid
55. TEMAZEPAM		7-chloro-1,3-dihydro-3-hydroxy-1-methyl-5-phenyl-2*H*-1,4-benzo-diazepin-2-one
56. TETRAZEPAM		7-chloro-5-(1-cyclohexen-1-yl)-1,3-dihydro-1-methyl-2*H*-1,4-benzo-diazepin-2-one
57. TRIAZOLAM		8-chloro-6-(*o*-chlorophenyl)-1-methyl-4*H*-*s*-triazolo[4,3-*a*][1,4]benzodiazepine
58. VINYLBITAL		5-(1-methylbutyl)-5-vinylbarbituric acid

The salts of the substances listed in this Schedule whenever the existence of such salts is possible.

United Nations Convention against Illicit Traffic in Narcotic Drugs and Psychotropic Substances 1988

(Vienna Convention)

The Vienna Convention was ratified by the United Kingdom on June 28, 1991 and came into force for the United Kingdom on September 26, 1991 (Cm. 1927).

The precursors listed in Annex E to the Convention have increased in number. They have been set out in the Table at para. 10.10 *ante*.

The Extradition (Drug Trafficking) Order 1991

(S.I. No. 1701)

Made	*24th July 1991*
Laid before Parliament	*1st August 1991*
Coming into force	*26th September 1991*

Now, therefore, Her Majesty, in exercise of the powers conferred upon Her by sections 2 and 21 of the Extradition Act 1870, and sections 4(1), 22(3) and 37(3) of the Extradition Act 1989 or otherwise in Her Majesty vested, is pleased by and with the advice of Her Privy Council, to order, and it is hereby ordered, as follows:-

1. This Order may be cited as the Extradition (Drug Trafficking) Order 1991, and shall come into force on 26th September 1991.

2. Schedule 1 to the Extradition Act 1989 ("the 1989 Act") shall apply in the case of a State mentioned in Schedule 2 to this Order under and in accordance with the extradition treaties listed in the second column of that Schedule as supplemented by paragraph 2 of Article 6 of the Convention (set out in Schedule 1 to this Order); the Orders in Council which give effect to the said extradition treaties shall be construed accordingly. The Convention entered into force for those States on the dates specified in the third column of the said Schedule 2.

3. The 1989 Act, so far as it relates to extradition procedures under Part III of that Act, shall apply in the case of a State mentioned in Part I of Schedule 3 to this Order (being States in respect of which the Convention entered into force on the dates specified in the second column of Part I of that Schedule) subject to the limitations, restrictions, exceptions and qualifications contained in Part II of that Schedule.

4. The operation of this Order is limited to the United Kingdom.

G. I. de Deney
Clerk of the Privy Council

SCHEDULE 1

CONVENTION AGAINST ILLICIT TRAFFIC IN NARCOTIC DRUGS AND PSYCHOTROPIC
SUBSTANCES

(Set out in Appendix XXII of the main work)

SCHEDULE 2   Article 2

FOREIGN STATES WHICH ARE PARTIES TO THE CONVENTION AND FOR WHICH ORDERS
UNDER THE EXTRADITION ACT 1870 ARE IN FORCE

State	Date of Extradition Treaty	Date of entry into force of Convention
Bolivia	22nd February 1892	18th November 1990
Chile	26th January 1897	11th November 1990
Ecuador	20th September 1880	11th November 1990
Guatemala	4th July 1885	29th May 1991
Mexico	7th September 1886	11th November 1990
Nicaragua	19th April 1905	11th November 1990
Paraguay	12th September 1908	21st November 1990
United States of America	8th June 1972	11th November 1990
Yugoslavia	6th December 1990	3rd April 1991

SCHEDULE 3   Article 3

PART I

FOREIGN STATES WHICH ARE PARTIES TO THE CONVENTION AND WITH WHICH NO
EXTRADITION TREATIES ARE IN FORCE

State	Date of entry into force of Convention
Bahrain	11th November 1990
Bhutan	25th November 1990
China	11th November 1990
Costa Rica	9th May 1991
Egypt	13th June 1991
Guinea	26th March 1991
Jordan	11th November 1990
Madagascar	10th June 1991
Oman	13th June 1991
Qatar	11th November 1990

State	Date of entry into force of Convention
Senegal	11th November 1990
Togo	11th November 1990
Tunisia	19th December 1990
United Arab Emirates	11th November 1990
Union of Soviet Socialist Republics	17th March 1991
Byelorussian Soviet Socialist Republic	13th January 1991

PART II

APPLICATION OF THE 1989 ACT IN THE CASE OF A STATE MENTIONED IN PART I

1. The 1989 Act shall hereby have effect only in respect of—
   (a) an offence mentioned in section 22(4)(h) of that Act;
   (b) an attempt to commit such an offence;
   (c) counselling, procuring, commanding, aiding or abetting such an offence; and
   (d) being an accessory before or after the fact to such an offence.

2. No proceeding shall be taken on an application for a provisional warrant issued under section 8(1)(b) of the 1989 Act, and no such warrant shall be issued, unless the application is made with the consent of the Secretary of State signified by an Order in the form set out in Part III of this Schedule or in a form to the like effect; but subject as aforesaid the signification of consent shall not affect the provisions of the said section 8.

3. (1) Without prejudice to his so deciding on other grounds, the Secretary of State may, in the circumstances mentioned in the following sub-paragraph, decide not to make an order or issue a warrant—
   (a) under section 7 of the 1989 Act issuing an authority to proceed, or
   (b) under section 12 of the 1989 Act ordering the person to be returned, or
   (c) for the purposes of paragraph 2 above signifying his consent to an application for a provisional warrant.

(2) The circumstances referred to in the preceding sub-paragraph are—
   (a) that the Secretary of State is not satisfied that provision is made by the law of the State requesting the return under which a person accused or convicted in the United Kingdom of the like offence as that with which the person whose return is sought is accused or convicted might be surrendered to the United Kingdom if found in that State, or
   (b) that the person whose return is sought is a British citizen, a British Dependent Territories citizen, a British Overseas citizen, a British subject, a British National (Overseas), or a British protected person.

PART III

FORM OF CONSENT OF SECRETARY OF STATE TO APPLICATION FOR A PROVISIONAL WARRANT

Whereas AB, a person recognised by the Secretary of State as a diplomatic or consular representative of   , has requested consent to application

being made for the issue of a provisional warrant for the arrest of CD, late of,
who [is accused] [has been convicted] of the commission of an offence
or attempt to commit an offence or counselling, procuring, commanding, aiding
or abetting an offence or of being accessory before or after the fact to an offence,
within the jurisdiction of the said State, being an offence which if committed in the
United Kingdom would be [a drug trafficking offence within the meaning of the
Drug Trafficking Offences Act 1986] [an offence to which section 1 of the
Criminal Justice (Scotland) Act 1987 relates].

By this Order the Secretary of State signifies to you his consent to the said
application being made.

Given under the hand of the undersigned, [one of Her Majesty's Principal
Secretaries of State] Minister of State at   ] [Under Secretary of State
at   ] this   day of   19   .

APPENDIX XXVI

Powers of Criminal Courts Act 1973

(CHAPTER 62)

Sched. 1A, para. 6

This Schedule was inserted by the Criminal Justice Act 1991, s.9(2).

Requirements as to treatment for drug or alcohol dependency

6.—(1) This paragraph applies where a court proposing to make a probation order is satisfied—

   (a) that the offender is dependent on drugs or alcohol;

   (b) that his dependency caused or contributed to the offence in respect of which the order is proposed to be made; and

   (c) that his dependency is such as requires and may be susceptible to treatment.

(2) The probation order may include a requirement that the offender shall submit, during the whole of the probation period or during such part of that period as may be specified in the order, to treatment by or under the direction of a person having the necessary qualifications or experience with a view to the reduction or elimination of the offender's dependency on drugs or alcohol.

(3) The treatment required by any such order shall be such one of the following kinds of treatment as may be specified in the order, that is to say—

   (a) treatment as a resident in such institution or place as may be specified in the order;

   (b) treatment as a non-resident in or at such institution or place as may be so specified; and

   (c) treatment by or under the direction of such person having the necessary qualifications or experience as may be so specified;

but the nature of the treatment shall not be specified in the order except as mentioned in paragraph (a), (b) or (c) above.

(4) A court shall not by virtue of this paragraph include in a probation order a requirement that the offender shall submit to treatment for his dependency on drugs or alcohol unless it is satisfied that arrangements have been made for the treatment intended to be specified in the order (including arrangements for the reception of the offender where he is to be required to submit to treatment as a resident).

(5) While the offender is under treatment as a resident in pursuance of a requirement of the probation order, the probation officer responsible for his supervision shall carry out the supervision to such extent only as may be necessary for the purpose of the revocation or amendment of the order.

(6) Where the person by whom or under whose direction an offender is being treated for dependency on drugs or alcohol in pursuance of a probation order is of the opinion that part of the treatment can be better or more conveniently given in or at an institution or place which—

    (a) is not specified in the order; and

    (b) is one in or at which the treatment of the offender will be given by or under the direction of a person having the necessary qualifications or experience he may, with the consent of the offender, make arrangements for him to be treated accordingly.

(7) Such arrangements as are mentioned in sub-paragraph (6) above may provide for the offender to receive part of his treatment as a resident in an institution or place notwithstanding that the institution or place is not one which could have been specified for that purpose in the probation order.

(8) Where any such arrangements as are mentioned in sub-paragraph (6) above are made for the treatment of an offender—

    (a) the person by whom the arrangements are made shall give notice in writing to the probation officer responsible for the supervision of the offender, specifying the institution or place in or at which the treatment is to be carried out; and

    (b) the treatment provided for by the arrangements shall be deemed to be treatment to which he is required to submit in pursuance of the probation order.

(9) In this paragraph the reference to the offender being dependent on drugs or alcohol includes a reference to his having a propensity towards the misuse of drugs or alcohol, and references to his dependency on drugs or alcohol shall be construed accordingly."

Practice Direction Rules Made by the Crown Court at Isleworth Pursuant to Section 1 of the Drug Trafficking Offences Act 1986

1. In any case in which the Prosecutor applies to the High Court for a Restraint or Charging Order under the Act and such an order is made, a copy thereof shall be provided to the Court as soon after committal as is practicable.

2. Rule 25A (1) of the Crown Court (Amendment) Rules 1986 provides that where in any proceedings in respect of a Drug Trafficking Offence, the Prosecutor or the defendant proposes to tender to the Crown any statement under Section 3 of the Act he shall give a copy thereof as soon as practicable to the defendant or the Prosecutor as the case may be and as soon after committal as practicable to the Appropriate Officer of the Crown Court, and in any event before the case appears in a Warned List.

3. (a) The above provision shall apply to all cases committed to this Court to which section 1(2) of the said Act may be held to apply.

(b) save those which involve defendants whose assets for the purposes of section 1(2) of the said Act are believed to be in excess of £2,000, when the following Directions shall apply.

4. The Prosecutor shall notify the Appropriate Officer of the Court (appointed under Rule 25A(1) Crown Court (Amendment) Rules 1986, and the Defence Solicitor or defendant if unrepresented, when he considers that paragraph 3(b) above may apply, and the Prosecutor shall provide the Crown Court with a Statement under section 3(1) (a) of the said Act with copies thereof to the persons named in Practice Directions *No: 2 above* all within the time limit therein provided.

Where a statement is tendered to the Court by the Prosecutor in which Practice Direction 3(b) applies, the defence Solicitor or the Defendant when unrepresented, shall if required and ordered by the Court, notification of which will be given by the Appropriate Officer aforesaid, file within 21 days of the said order, a Counter-Notice by reason of section 3(2) of the aforementioned Act and Rule 25A of the Crown Court (Amendment) Rules 1986, indicating to the Court and the Prosecution to what extent the Defence accepts each allegation and statement and, so far as they, or the Defendant, when unrepresented, does not accept any such allegations to provide an indication of the matters it is proposed to rely on.

5. Where the Defence Solicitor, or if unrepresented, the defendant, contend that they or he, are unable to supply a Counter-Notice as envisaged by section 3(2) of the said Act within the time limit set out in Direction No:2 above, or wish to submit that the defendant should not be required to supply a Counter-Notice, application may be made to the Court on Notice in writing, with a copy to the Prosecutor, within the time period referred to in the Courts' original Order for supplying the Counter-Notice. The Prosecutor shall attend to respond to the application, which the Court shall arrange, and which may at the request of either party be treated by the Court as a Pre-Trial Review and Directions, and upon such application the Court may make such order as it thinks fit as to time-limits for delivery of Counter-Notices and any other Direction it sees fit to make.

6. The Prosecutor is required at the time of serving a section 3 statement, or at the time of reviewing a Counter-Notice to indicate to the Court whether or not in his view, it is appropriate for the Court to serve copies of any document or notice on any third party who might be affected by the making of a Confiscation Order, since the Court shall have to consider the position of such parties and their possible legal representation on the hearing of the substantive matter and before a Confiscation Order is made. The Court may, through the Appropriate Officer, indicate what information, if any, shall be provided to third parties.

The Criminal Justice (International Co-operation) Act 1990 (Designation of Prosecuting Authorities) Order 1991

(S.I. No. 1224)

Made	*21st May 1991*
Coming into force	*10th June 1991*

In exercise of the power conferred upon me by section 3(3) of the Criminal Justice (International Co-operation) Act 1990 I hereby make the following Order:

1. This Order may be cited as the Criminal Justice (International Co-operation) Act 1990 (Designation of Prosecuting Authorities) Order 1991 and shall come into force on 10th June 1991.

2. The prosecuting authorities specified in the Schedule to this Order are hereby designated for the purposes of section 3 of the Criminal Justice (International Co-operation) Act 1990.

SCHEDULE   Article 2

Designated Prosecuting Authority

The Attorney General for England and Wales
The Director of Public Prosecutions and any Crown Prosecutor
The Director of the Serious Fraud Office and any person designated under section
    1(7) of the Criminal Justice Act 1987
The Secretary of State for Trade and Industry
The Commissioners of Customs and Excise
The Lord Advocate
Any Procurator Fiscal
The Attorney General for Northern Ireland
The Director of Public Prosecutions for Northern Ireland

The Crown Court (Amendment) Rules 1991

(S.I. No. 1288 (L.13))

Made	*27th May 1991*
Laid before Parliament	*10th June 1991*
Coming into force	*1st July 1991*

We, the Crown Court Rule Committee, in exercise of the powers conferred upon us by sections 84(1) and 86 of the Supreme Court Act 1981, and section 10 of the Criminal Justice (International Co-operation) Act 1990, hereby make the following Rules:

1. These Rules may be cited as the Crown Court (Amendment) Rules 1991 and shall come into force on 1st July 1991.

2. The Crown Court Rules 1982 shall be amended by the insertion after rule 29 of the following rules:

"Service of summons or order outside the United Kingdom

30. Where a witness summons or order is issued or made by the Crown Court in accordance with section 2(1) of the Criminal Justice (International Co-operation) Act 1990 for service outside the United Kingdom it shall be sent forthwith by the appropriate officer of the Crown Court to the Secretary of State with a view to its being served there in accordance with arrangements made by the Secretary of State.

Application for letters of request

31.—(1) Notice of an application under section 3(1) of the Criminal Justice (International Co-operation) Act 1990 (overseas evidence for use in the United Kingdom) shall be given to the appropriate officer of the Crown Court and shall—

    (a) be made in writing, save that the court may in exceptional circumstances dispense with the need for notice;

    (b) state the particulars of the offence which it is alleged has been committed or the grounds upon which it is suspected that an offence has been committed;

    (c) state whether proceedings in respect of the offence have been instituted or the offence is being investigated;

(d) include particulars of the assistance requested in the form of a draft letter of request.

(2) The application may be heard ex parte.

(3) When hearing the application the court may, if it thinks it necessary in the interests of justice, direct that the public be excluded from the court.

(4) The powers conferred on the Crown Court by paragraph (3) above shall be in addition and without prejudice to any other powers of the court to hear proceedings in camera.

(5) Where in a case of urgency the Crown Court sends a letter of request direct to any court or tribunal in accordance with section 3(5) of the Criminal Justice (International Co-operation) Act 1990, the appropriate officer of the Crown Court shall forthwith notify the Secretary of State of this and send with the notification a copy of the letter of request.

Proceedings before a nominated court

32.—(1) Where the Crown Court receives evidence in proceedings before a nominated court in pursuance of a notice under section 4(2) of the Criminal Justice (International Co-operation) Act 1990 the court may, if it thinks it necessary in the interest of justice, direct that the public be excluded from the court.

(2) The powers conferred on the Crown Court by paragraph (1) above shall be in addition and without prejudice to any other powers of the court to hear proceedings in camera.

(3) Where the Crown Court receives evidence in proceedings mentioned in paragraph (1) above the appropriate officer of the Crown Court shall make a record of—

(a) which persons with an interest in the proceedings were present;

(b) which of the said persons were represented and by whom;

(c) whether any of the said persons were denied the opportunity of cross-examining a witness as to any part of his testimony and the reasons for any such denial.

(4) When so requested by the Secretary of State, the appropriate officer of the Crown Court send to him a copy of the record as mentioned in paragraph (3) above.

Application for increase in term of imprisonment in default of payment— drug trafficking

33.—(1) The following provisions of this rule shall have effect for the purposes of applications under subsection (2) of section 15 of the Criminal Justice (International Co-operation) Act 1990 (which provides for interest on sums unpaid under confiscation orders in drug trafficking cases).

(2) Notice of application under subsection (2) of the said section 15 to increase the term of imprisonment or detention fixed in default of payment of a confiscation order by a person ('the defendant') shall be made by the prosecutor in writing to the appropriate officer of the Crown Court.

(3) A notice under paragraph (2) above shall—

(a) state the name and address of the defendant;

(b) specify the grounds for the application;

(c) give details of the enforcement measures taken, if any; and

(d) include a copy of the confiscation order.

(4) On receiving a notice under paragraph (2) above, the appropriate officer of the Crown Court shall—
  (a) forthwith send to the defendant and the magistrates' court required to enforce payment of the confiscation order under section 32(1) of the Powers of Criminal Courts Act 1973, a copy of the said notice; and
  (b) notify in writing the applicant and the defendant of the date, time and place appointed for the hearing of the application.

(5) Where the Crown Court makes an order pursuant to an application mentioned in paragraph (1) above, the appropriate officer of the Crown Court shall send forthwith a copy of the order—
  (a) to the applicant;
  (b) to the defendant;
  (c) where the defendant is at the time of the making of the order in custody, to the person having custody of him; and
  (d) to the magistrates' court mentioned in paragraph (4)(a) above.".

APPENDIX XXX

The Criminal Justice (International Co-operation) Act 1990 (Exercise of Powers) Order 1991

(S.I. No. 1297)

Made	*4th June 1991*
Laid before Parliament	*7th June 1991*
Coming into force	*1st July 1991*

The Treasury, in exercise of the powers conferred on them by sections 7(7) and 8(5) of the Criminal Justice (International Co-operation) Act 1990, hereby make the following Order:

1. This Order may be cited as the Criminal Justice (International Co-operation) Act 1990 (Exercise of Powers) Order 1991 and shall come into operation on 1st July 1991.

2. In this Order—

"the Act" means the Criminal Justice (International Co-operation) Act 1990;

"officer" means a person commissioned by the Commissioners of Customs and Excise under section 6(3) of the Customs and Excise Management Act 1979.

3. In England and Wales and Northern Ireland, any powers exercisable by a constable under section 7 of the Act, shall also be exercisable by an officer or by any person acting under the direction of an officer.

4. In Scotland, any powers to enter, search or seize granted under section 8(1) of the Act shall also be exercisable by an offer or by any person acting under the direction of an officer.

The Criminal Justice (International Co-operation) Act 1990 (Enforcement of Overseas Forfeiture Orders) Order 1991

(S.I. No. 1463)

Made	*26 June 1991*
Coming into force	*1st July 1991*

Now, therefore, Her Majesty, in exercise of the powers conferred upon Her by section 9 of the Criminal Justice (International Co-operation) Act 1990, is pleased, by and with the advice of Her Privy Council, to order, and it is hereby ordered, as follows:

Title, commencement and extent

1.—(1) This Order may be cited as the Criminal Justice (International Co-operation) Act 1990 (Enforcement of Overseas Forfeiture Orders) Order 1991 and shall come into force on 1st July 1991.

(2) This Order extends to England and Wales only.

Interpretation

2.—(1) In this Order—

"a court of a designated country" includes a court of any state or territory of a designated country;

"appropriate authority of a designated country" means—

(a) the authority specified opposite that country in Schedule 2 to this Order, or

(b) where no authority is so specified, the authority appearing to the court to be the appropriate authority for the purposes of this Order;

"constable" includes a person commissioned by the Commissioners of Customs and Excise;

"designated country" means a country or territory designated under article 4 of this Order;

"drug trafficking offence" means any offence corresponding to or similar to—

(a) an offence under section 4(2) or (3) or 5(3) of the Misuse of Drugs Act 1971 (production, supply and possession for supply of controlled drugs);
(b) an offence under section 20 of that Act (assisting in or inducing commission outside United Kingdom of an offence punishable under a corresponding law);
(c) an offence under—
    (i) section 50(2) or (3) of the Customs and Excise Management Act 1979 (improper importation),
    (ii) section 68(2) of that Act (exportation), or
    (iii) section 170 of that Act (fraudulent evasion),
    in connection with a prohibition or restriction on importation or exportation having effect by virtue of section 3 of the Misuse of Drugs Act 1971;
(d) an offence under section 24 of the Drug Trafficking Offences Act 1986;
(e) an offence under section 12, 14 or 19 of the 1990 Act;
(f) an offence under section 1 of the Criminal Law Act 1977 of conspiracy to commit any of the offences in paragraphs (a) to (e) above;
(g) an offence under section 1 of the Criminal Attempts Act 1981 of attempting to commit any of those offences;
(h) an offence of inciting another to commit any of those offences, whether under section 19 of the Misuse of Drugs Act 1971 or at common law; and
(i) aiding, abetting, counselling or procuring the commission of any of those offences;
"property" includes money and all other property, real or personal, heritable or moveable, including things in action and other intangible or incorporeal property;
"the 1990 Act" means the Criminal Justice (International Co-operation) Act 1990.

(2) This Order applies to property whether it is situated in England or Wales or elsewhere.

(3) The following provisions shall have effect for the interpretation of this Order.

(4) Property is held by any person if he holds any interest in it.

(5) Proceedings are instituted in a designated country when—
(a) under the law of the designated country concerned one of the steps specified in relation to that country in the right-hand column of Schedule 1 to this Order has been taken there in respect of an alleged drug trafficking offence; or
(b) an application has been made to a court in a designated country for an external forfeiture order,
and where the application of this paragraph would result in there being more than one time for the institution of proceedings, they shall be taken to have been instituted at the earliest of those times.

(6) Proceedings are concluded—
(a) when (disregarding any power of a court to grant leave to appeal out of time) there is no further possibility of a forfeiture order being made in the proceedings;
(b) on the satisfaction of a forfeiture order made in the proceedings

(whether by the recovery of all property liable to be recovered, or otherwise).

(7) An order is subject to appeal until (disregarding any power of a court to grant leave to appeal out of time) there is no further possibility of an appeal on which the order could be varied or set aside.

External forfeiture orders

3.—(1) An order made by a court in a designated country for the forfeiture and destruction or forfeiture and other disposal, of anything in respect of which a drug trafficking offence has been committed or which was used in connection with the commission of such an offence is referred to in this Order as an "external forfeiture order".

(2) In paragraph (1) above the reference to an order includes any order, decree, direction or judgment, or any part thereof, however described.

(3) A person against whom an external forfeiture order has been made, or a person against whom proceedings which may result in an external forfeiture order being made have been, or are to be, instituted in a court in a designated country, is referred to as "the defendant".

Designation of countries and territories

4. Each of the countries and territories specified in Schedule 2 to this Order is hereby designated for the purposes of section 9 of the 1990 Act.

Restraint orders

5.—(1) The High Court may in accordance with this paragraph by an order (referred to in this Order as a "restraint order") prohibit any person, subject to such conditions and exceptions as may be specified in the order, from dealing with any property liable to forfeiture, that is to say, any property in respect of which an external forfeiture order has been made or in respect of which such an order could be made in the proceedings referred to in paragraphs (2) or (3) below.

(2) A restraint order may be made where—

- (a) proceedings have been instituted against the defendant in a designated country,
- (b) the proceedings have not been concluded, and
- (c) either an external forfeiture order has been made in the proceedings or it appears to the High Court that there are reasonable grounds for believing that such an order may be made in them.

(3) A restraint order may also be made where—

- (a) it appears to the High Court that proceedings are to be instituted against the defendant in a designated country; and
- (b) it appears to the court that there are reasonable grounds for believing that an external forfeiture order may be made in them.

(4) Where the court has made an order under paragraph (1) above by virtue of paragraph (3) above, the court shall discharge the order if the proposed proceedings are not instituted within such time as the court considers reasonable.

(5) A restraint order—

- (a) may be made only on an application by or on behalf of the government of a designated country or, in a case where an external forfeiture order has been registered under article 10 of this Order, by a Crown Prosecutor or a person authorised in that behalf by the Commissioners of Customs and Excise,

(b) may be made on an ex parte application to a judge in chambers, and

(c) notwithstanding anything in Order 11 of the Rules of the Supreme Court may provide for service on, or the provision of notice to, persons affected by the order in such manner as the High Court may direct.

(6) A restraint order—

(a) may be discharged or varied in relation to any property, and

(b) shall be discharged when the proceedings in relation to which the order was made are concluded.

(7) An application for the discharge or variation of a restraint order may be made by any person affected by it.

(8) Where the High Court has made a restraint order, the court may at any time appoint a receiver—

(a) to take possession of any property specified in the restraint order, and

(b) in accordance with the court's directions, to manage or otherwise deal with any property in respect of which he is appointed,

subject to such exceptions and conditions as may be specified by the court, and may require any person having possession of property in respect of which a receiver is appointed under this article to give possession of it to the receiver.

(9) For the purposes of this article, dealing with property held by any person includes (without prejudice to the generality of the expression) removing the property from England and Wales.

(10) Where a restraint order has been made, a constable may for the purpose of preventing any property specified in the restraint order being removed from England and Wales seize the property.

(11) Property seized under paragraph (10) above shall be dealt with in accordance with the directions of the court which made the order.

Applications for restraint orders

6. An application under article 5(5) of this Order shall be supported by an affidavit which shall—

(a) state, where applicable the grounds for believing that an external forfeiture order may be made in the proceedings instituted or to be instituted in the designated country concerned;

(b) to the best of the deponent's ability, give particulars of the property in respect of which the order is sought and specify the person or persons holding such property;

(c) in a case to which article 5(3) of this Order applies, indicate when it is intended that proceedings should be instituted in the designated country concerned,

and the affidavit may, unless the court otherwise directs, contain statements of information or belief with the sources and grounds thereof.

Disposal of forfeited property

7.—(1) Where an external forfeiture order has been registered in the High Court under article 10 of this Order, the High Court may, on the application of a Crown Prosecutor or a person authorised in that behalf by the Commissioners of Customs and Excise, order the forfeiture of the property specified in the external forfeiture order.

(2) Property forfeited under paragraph (1) above shall be disposed of in accordance with the courts' directions.

(3) The court shall not in respect of any property exercise the powers conferred by paragraphs (1) and (2) above unless a reasonable opportunity has been given for persons holding any interest in the property to make representations to the court.

Exercise of powers by High Court or receiver

8.—(1) This article applies to the powers conferred on the High Court by articles 5 and 7 above or on a receiver appointed under article 5 of this Order.

(2) The powers shall be exercised with a view to recovering property which is liable to be recovered under an external forfeiture order registered in the High Court under article 10 of this Order or, as the case may be, with a view to recovering property which may become liable to be recovered under any external forfeiture order which may be made in the defendant's case.

Receivers: supplementary provisions

9.—(1) Where a receiver appointed under article 5 of this Order takes any action—
- (a) in relation to property which is not liable to recovery under an external forfeiture order, being action which he would be entitled to take if it were such property,
- (b) believing, and having reasonable grounds for believing, that he is entitled to take that action in relation to that property,

he shall not be liable to any person in respect of any loss or damage resulting from his action except in so far as the loss or damage is caused by his negligence.

(2) Any amount due in respect of the remuneration and expenses of a receiver so appointed shall be paid by the person on whose application the receiver was appointed.

Registration of external forfeiture orders

10.—(1) On an application made by or on behalf of the government of a designated country, the High Court may register an external forfeiture order made there if—
- (a) it is satisfied that at the time of registration the order is in force and not subject to appeal;
- (b) it is satisfied, where the person against whom the order is made did not appear in the proceedings, that he received notice of the proceedings in sufficient time to enable him to defend them; and
- (c) it is of the opinion that enforcing the order in England and Wales would not be contrary to the interests of justice.

(2) In paragraph (1) above "appeal" includes—
- (a) any proceedings by way of discharging or setting aside a judgment; and
- (b) an application for a new trial or a stay of execution.

(3) The High Court shall cancel the registration of an external forfeiture order if it appears to the court that the order has been satisfied by the forfeiture of the

property liable to be recovered under the external forfeiture order or by any other means.

Proof of orders and judgment of court in a designated country

11.—(1) For the purposes of this Order—
(a) any order made or judgment given by a court in a designated country purporting to bear the seal of that court, or to be signed by any person in his capacity as a judge, magistrate or officer of the court, shall be deemed without further proof to have been duly sealed or, as the case may be, to have been signed by that person; and
(b) a document, duly authenticated, which purports to be a copy of any order made or judgment given by a court in a designated country shall be deemed without further proof to be a true copy.

(2) A document purporting to be a copy of any order made or judgment given by a court in a designated country is duly authenticated for the purposes of paragraph (1)(b) above if it purports to be certified by any person in his capacity as a judge, magistrate or officer of the court in question or by or on behalf of the appropriate authority of the designated country.

Evidence in relation to proceedings and orders in a designated country

12.—(1) For the purposes of this Order, a certificate purporting to be issued by or on behalf of the appropriate authority of a designated country stating—
(a) that proceedings have been instituted and have not been concluded, or that proceedings are to be instituted, there;
(b) that an external forfeiture order is in force and is not subject to appeal;
(c) that property recoverable in the designated country under an external forfeiture order remains unrecovered there;
(d) that any person has been notified of any proceedings in accordance with the law of the designated country; or
(e) that an order (however described) made by a court of the designated country is for the forfeiture and destruction or the forfeiture and other disposal of anything in respect of which a drug trafficking offence has been committed or which was used in connection with the commission of such an offence,
shall, in any proceedings in the High Court, be admissible as evidence of the facts so stated.

(2) In any such proceedings a statement contained in a document, duly authenticated, which purports to have been received in evidence or to be a copy of a document so received, or to set out or summarise evidence given in proceedings in a court in a designated country, shall be admissible as evidence of any fact stated therein.

(3) A document is duly authenticated for the purposes of paragraph (2) above if it purports to be certified by any person in his capacity as judge, magistrate or officer of the court in the designated country, or by or on behalf of the appropriate authority of the designated country, to have been received in evidence or to be a copy of a document so received, or, as the case may be, to be the original document containing or summarising the evidence or a true copy of that document.

(4) Nothing in this article shall prejudice the admission of any evidence,

whether contained in any document or otherwise, which is admissible apart from this article.

Certificate of appropriate authority

13. Where in relation to any designated country no authority is specified in Schedule 2 to this Order, a certificate made by the Secretary of State to the effect that the authority specified therein is the appropriate authority for the purposes of this Order shall be sufficient evidence of that fact.

Representation of government of a designated country

14. A request for assistance sent to the Secretary of State by the appropriate authority of a designated country shall, unless the contrary is shown, be deemed to constitute the authority of the government of that country for the Crown Prosecution Service or the Commissioners of Customs and Excise to act on its behalf in any proceedings in the High Court under article 10 or any other provision of this Order.

SCHEDULE 1   Article 2(5)

INSTITUTION OF PROCEEDINGS

Designated country	*Point at which proceedings are instituted*
Anguilla	(a) when a summons or warrant is issued in respect of an offence; (b) when a person is charged with an offence after being taken into custody without a warrant; (c) when a bill of indictment is preferred
Australia	(a) when an information has been laid before a justice of the peace; (b) when a person is charged with an offence after having been taken into custody without a warrant; (c) when a bill of indictment is preferred
the Bahamas	(a) when an information has been laid before a justice of the peace; (b) when a person is charged with an offence after having been taken into custody without a warrant; (c) when a bill of indictment is preferred
Bahrain	when a bill of indictment is lodged in court against any person for an offence
Barbados	(a) when an information has been laid before a magistrate; (b) when a person is charged with an offence; (c) when a bill of indictment is preferred
Bermuda	when an information is laid charging a person with an offence

Designated country	Point at which proceedings are instituted
the Cayman Islands	(a) when a charge has been signed under subsection (3) or (4) of section 13 of the Criminal Procedure Code in respect of the offence; or (b) when a person is charged with the offence after being arrested without a warrant under subsection (5) of that section
Gibraltar	when a person is charged with an offence, whether by the laying of an information or otherwise
Guernsey	when a person is charged with an offence
Hong Kong	(a) when a magistrate issues a warrant or summons; (b) when a person is charged with an offence; (c) when an indictment is preferred
Isle of Man	(a) where a justice of the peace issues a summons under section 4 of the Summary Jurisdiction Act 1989, when the complaint in relation to the offence is made to him; (b) where a justice of the peace issues a warrant for the arrest of any person under that section, when the complaint in relation to the offence is made to him; (c) where a person is charged with the offence after being taken into custody without a warrant, when he is taken into custody; (d) where an information is preferred by the Attorney General in a case where there have been no comittal proceedings, when the information is lodged in the General Registry in accordance with section 4(1) of the Criminal Code Amendment Act 1917
Italy	(a) when a person is notified, in accordance with article 369 of the Italian Code of Criminal Procedure, that a prosecution against him is in progress; (b) when a proposal for the application of a preventative measure ("*misura di prevenzione*") is laid before a court
Jersey	(a) when the Bailiff issues a warrant in respect of an offence for the arrest of a person who is out of the island; (b) when a person is arrested and charged with an offence; (c) when a summons in respect of an offence is served on a person at the instance of the Attorney General;

Designated country	Point at which proceedings are instituted
	(d) when a summons in respect of the offence is served on a person in accordance with the provisions of Article 8 of the Police Court (Miscellaneous Provisions) (Jersey) Law, 1949
Malaysia	when a person is charged with an offence
Montserrat	(a) when a judge issues a summons or warrant in respect of an offence;
	(b) when a person is charged with an offence after being taken into custody without a warrant
Saudi Arabia	when an information has been laid before a judicial authority
Spain	when by virtue of a judicial resolution it is decided to proceed against a person for an offence
Sweden	when a public prosecutor has established that there are reasonable grounds to suspect that a person has committed an offence and accordingly is obliged under the Code of Judicial Procedure to notify the person of the suspicion
Switzerland	when proceedings for an offence are brought before an examining magistrate
United Mexican States	when criminal proceedings are instituted by a judicial authority
United States of America	when an indictment, information or complaint has been filed against a person in respect of an offence

SCHEDULE 2 Article 4

Designated country	Appropriate authority
Anguilla	the Attorney General of Anguilla
Australia	the Attorney General's Department
the Bahamas	the Attorney General of the Bahamas
Bahrain	the Ministry of the Interior
Bangladesh	
Barbados	the Attorney General
Bermuda	the Attorney General of Bermuda
Bhutan	
Bolivia	
Canada	the Minister of Justice or officials designated by that Minister
the Cayman Islands	the Attorney General of the Cayman Islands

Designated country	*Appropriate authority*
Chile	
China	
Costa Rica	
Cyprus	
Ecuador	
Egypt	
France	
Ghana	
Gibraltar	the Attorney General of Gibraltar
Grenada	
Guatemala	
Guernsey	Her Majesty's Attorney General for the Bailiwick of Guernsey
Guinea	
Hong Kong	the Attorney General of Hong Kong
India	the Ministry of Home Affairs
Isle of Man	Her Majesty's Attorney General for the Isle of Man
Italy	the Ministry of Justice
Jersey	Her Majesty's Attorney General for the Bailiwick of Jersey
Jordan	
Madagascar	
Malaysia	the Inspector General of Police, Malaysia
Montserrat	the Attorney General of Montserrat
Nicaragua	
Nigeria	the Attorney General of the Federation of the Republic of Nigeria
Oman	
Paraguay	
Qatar	
Saudi Arabia	the Ministry of the Interior
Senegal	
Spain	the Ministerio de Justicia, Madrid
Sweden	the Ministry for Foreign Affairs
Switzerland	the Eidgenössisches Justiz und Polizeidepartement
Togo	
Tunisia	
Uganda	
Union of Soviet Socialist Republics (including the Byelorussian Soviet Socialist Republic)	
United Arab Emirates	
United Mexican States	the Office of the Attorney General
United States of America	the Attorney General of the United States of America
Yugoslavia	

The Drug Trafficking Offences Act 1986 (Designated Countries and Territories) (Amendment) Order 1991

(S.I. No. 1465)

Made	*26th June 1991*
Coming into force	*1st July 1991*

Whereas a draft of this Order has been approved by a resolution of each House of Parliament:

Now, therefore, Her Majesty, in exercise of the powers conferred upon Her by section 26 of the Drug Trafficking Offences Act 1986, is pleased, by and with the advice of Her Privy Council, to order, and it is hereby ordered, as follows:

1.—(1) This Order may be cited as the Drug Trafficking Offences Act 1986 (Designated Countries and Territories) (Amendment) Order 1991 and shall come into force on the 1st July 1991.

(2) In this Order "the Act" means the Drug Trafficking Offences Act 1986 and "the principal Order" means the Drug Trafficking Offences Act 1986 (Designated Countries and Territories) Order 1990.

2. In article 2 of the principal Order for the definition of "appropriate authority of a designated country" there shall be substituted the following definition—

" "appropriate authority of a designated country" means—

(a) the authority specified opposite that country in Schedule 1 to this Order, or

(b) where no authority is so specified, the authority appearing to the court to be the appropriate authority of that country for the purposes of section 26 and 26A of the Act, and of the other provisions of the Act as applied under article 3(2) of this Order;"

3. After article 5 of the principle Order there shall be inserted the following article:

"Certificate as to appropriate authority of a designated country

5A. Where in relation to any designated country no authority is specified in Schedule 1 to this Order, a certificate made by the Secretary of State to the effect that the authority specified therein is the appropriate authority for the purposes of section 26 and 26A of the Act, and of the other provisions of the

106

Act as applied by article 3(2) of this Order shall be sufficient evidence of that
fact".

4. Schedule 1 to the principal Order shall be amended by inserting in
alphabetical order the entries for those countries and territories specified in the
Schedule to this Order.

5.—(1) In paragraph 11(a) of Schedule 2 to the principal Order for "(3)" there
shall be substituted "(4)".

(2) In paragraph 12(1) of Schedule 3 to the principal Order for "(3)" there shall
be substituted "(4)".

6. The Appendix set out at the end of Schedule 3 to the principal Order (which
defines the institution of proceedings for the purposes of section 38(11) of the
Drug Trafficking Offences Act 1986 as modified by Schedule 2 to the principal
Order) shall be amended as follows:

(a) after the entry relating to the Bahamas, there shall be inserted the
following—

> "Bahrain — when a bill of indictment is lodged in court against any person for an offence

> Barbados — (a) when an information has been laid before a magistrate;
> (b) when a person is charged with an offence;
> (c) when a bill of indictment is preferred;

(b) after the entry relating to Bermuda, there shall be inserted the
following—

> "the Cayman Islands — (a) when a charge has been signed under subsection (3) or (4) of section 13 of the Criminal Procedure Code in respect of the offence;
> (b) when a person is charged with the offence after being arrested without a warrant under subsection (5) of that section";

(c) after the entry relating to Guernsey, there shall be inserted the
following—

> "Hong Kong — (a) when a magistrate issues a warrant or summons;
> (b) when a person is charged with an offence;
> (c) when an indictment is preferred";

(d) in the entry relating to the Isle of Man, for the words "section 13 of the
Petty Sessions and Summary Jurisdiction Act 1927" there shall be
substituted the words "section 4 of the Summary Jurisdiction Act 1989";

(e) after the entry relating to the Isle of Man, there shall be inserted the
following—

"Italy   (a) when a person is notified, in
                                   accordance with article 369 of the
                                   Italian Code of Criminal Procedure,
                                   that a prosecution against him is in
                                   progress;
                               (b) when a proposal for the application
                                   of a preventative measure ("*misura
                                   di prevenzione*") is laid before a
                                   court"; and

(f) after the entry relating to Malaysia, there shall be inserted the
    following—

"Montserrat   (a) when a judge issues a summons or
                                   warrant in respect of an offence;
                               (b) when a person is charged with an
                                   offence after being taken into
                                   custody without a warrant

Saudi Arabia   when an information has been laid
                               before a judicial authority".

SCHEDULE   Article 2

Designated Country	*Appropriate authority*
Bahrain	the Ministry of the Interior
Bangladesh	
Barbados	the Attorney General
Bhutan	
Bolivia	
the Cayman Islands	the Attorney General of the Cayman Islands
Chile	
China	
Costa Rica	
Cyprus	
Ecuador	
Egypt	
France	
Ghana	
Guinea	
Grenada	
Guatemala	
Hong Kong	the Attorney General of Hong Kong
India	the Ministry of Home Affairs
Italy	the Ministry of Justice
Jordan	
Madagascar	
Montserrat	the Attorney General of Montserrat
Nicaragua	

Designated Country	*Appropriate authority*
Oman	
Paraguay	
Qatar	
Saudi Arabia	the Ministry of the Interior
Senegal	
Togo	
Tunisia	
Uganda	
Union of Soviet Socialist Republics (including the Byelorussian Soviet Socialist Republic)	
United Arab Emirates	
Yugoslavia	

The Magistrates' Courts (Detention and Forfeiture of Drug Trafficking Cash) Rules 1991

(S.I. No. 1923 (c.30))

Made	*21st August 1991*
Laid before Parliament	*2nd September 1991*
Coming into force	*23rd September 1991*

ARRANGEMENT OF RULES

The Lord Chancellor, in exercise of the power conferred on him by section 144 of the Magistrates' Courts Act 1980, after consultation with the Rule Committee appointed under the said section 144, hereby makes the following Rules:

Citation, commencement and interpretation

1.—(1) These Rules may be cited as the Magistrates' Courts (Detention and Forfeiture of Drug Trafficking Cash) Rules 1991, and shall come into force on 23rd September 1991.

(2) In these Rules—
- (a) "the Act" means the Criminal Justice (International Co-operation) Act 1990; and
- (b) any reference to a form is a reference to a form set out in the Schedule to these Rules or a form to the like effect.

Application for continued detention of seized cash

2.—(1) An application for an order under section 25(2) of the Act for continued detention of cash seized under section 25(1) thereof shall be made in writing in Form A to a justice of the peace who ordinarily acts for the petty sessions area in which the cash was seized.

(2) A copy of the written application under paragraph (1) above shall be given by the applicant to the person from whom the cash was seized.

Hearing of application for continued detention of seized cash

3.—(1) A justice of the peace considering an application under section 25(2) of the Act shall require the matters contained in it to be sworn by the applicant under oath, may require the applicant to answer any questions under oath, and may require any statement in response by the person from whom the cash was seized to be made under oath.

(2) The justice shall record or cause to be recorded in writing the substance of any statements made under oath which are not already recorded in the written application.

Unattended parcels etc.

4. In rules 2, 3 and 8 of these Rules, references to the person from whom the cash was seized include references to the sender and the intended recipient, where known, of a letter, parcel, container or other means of unattended dispatch, but a justice of the peace shall not decline to hear an application in such a case solely on the ground that it has not been proved that the sender or intended recipient has received a copy of the written application under rule 2(2) of these Rules.

Order for continued detention of seized cash

5.—(1) An order made by a justice of the peace under section 25(2) of the Act shall be in Form B.

(2) Notice of any order mentioned in paragraph (1) above shall be given forthwith by the applicant to any person appearing to him to be affected by it and such notice shall be in the form set out in Form B and shall be accompanied by a copy of the said order.

Notice of order for continued detention of seized cash

6. Where, in accordance with an order made under section 25(2) of the Act, the applicant gives notice to any person affected by the order, the applicant shall notify the clerk of the magistrates' court to which any application under section

25(3) or (5) would, in accordance with rule 7(1) and (2) of these Rules, be made of the names and addresses of the persons so notified.

Subsequent applications

7.—(1) An application under section 25(3) of the Act for further detention of cash shall be in Form C and shall be sent to the clerk to the justices for the petty sessions area in which the seizure was made.

(2) An application under section 25(5) of the Act for the release of detained cash shall be made in writing to the clerk of the said magistrates' court, and shall specify the grounds on which it is made.

(3) The clerk of the magistrates' court who receives an application in accordance with paragraph (1) or (2) above shall fix a date for the hearing of the application, shall notify the applicant thereof and shall notify any persons to whom notice of the order for continued detention has been given of the application and of the date fixed for the hearing.

(4) If the court is satisfied that an order for further detention of cash should be made under section 25(3) of the Act, it shall endorse the order for continued detention accordingly, and a copy of the order so endorsed shall be given by the clerk of the court to any persons to whom notice of the order for continued detention has been given.

Direction for release of cash

8. A direction under section 25(5)(a) of the Act for the release of detained cash shall be in Form D, and shall provide for the release of the cash within 7 days of the date of the making of the direction or such longer period as with the agreement of the person from whom the cash was seized may be specified in the notice.

Forfeiture

9.—(1) An application for forfeiture of cash under section 26 of the Act shall be in Form E and shall be addressed to the clerk of the magistrates' court referred to in rule 7(1) of these Rules.

(2) The clerk of the magistrates' court who receives such an application shall fix a date for the hearing, shall notify the applicant thereof, and shall notify any persons to whom notice of an order for continued detention has been given of the application and of the date fixed for the hearing.

Joinder

10. At any hearing under section 25(3) or (5) of the Act, or under section 26 thereof, or on the application of any person affected by an order for continued or further detention, the court may, if it thinks fit, order that such person be joined as a party to the proceedings and, if the court so orders, otherwise than at such a hearing, the clerk of the magistrates' court shall give notice to the other parties.

Notice

11. Any notice or copy of any order required to be given to any person under the foregoing provisions of these Rules may be given by post to his last known address.

Procedure at hearings

12.—(1) At the hearing of an application under section 25(3) or (5) of the Act, or under section 26 thereof, any person to whom notice of the application has been given may attend and be heard on the question whether a further order should be made, an existing order should be discharged, or a forfeiture order should be made, as the case may be, but the fact that any such person does not attend shall not prevent the court from hearing the application.

(2) Subject to the foregoing provisions of these Rules, proceedings on such an application shall be regulated in the same manner as proceedings on a complaint, and accordingly for the purposes of this rule the application shall be deemed to be a complaint, the applicant to be a complainant, the respondents to be defendants, and any notice given by the clerk to a magistrates' court under rule 7(3) or 9(2) of these Rules to be a summons; but nothing in this rule shall be construed as enabling a warrant of arrest to be issued for failure to appear in answer to any such notice.

SCHEDULE　　　　　　　　　　　　　Rule 1(2)(b)

FORMS

FORM A

Application for Continued Detention of Seized Cash (Criminal Justice (International Co-operation) Act 1990, s.25(2))

.... Magistrates' Court
.... Code

Date ....

Person from whom cash seized ....*

Address ....*

Amount seized (**estimated) ....

Date of seizure ....

Time of seizure ....

Place of seizure ....

(Name of applicant) ...., of ....
(address and official position of applicant)

....

applies for an order under section 25(2) of the Criminal Justice (International Co-operation) Act 1990 authorising the continued detention of the above-mentioned cash and will state upon oath that

(a) there are reasonable grounds for suspecting that it directly or indirectly represents any person's proceeds of, or is intended by any person for use in, drug trafficking, namely–
(state grounds) . . . .

. . . .

. . . .

and

(b) the continued detention of the cash for a period of . . . . is justified while–
   (i)   its origin or derivation is further investigated,**
   (ii) consideration is given to the institution of criminal proceedings against any person for an offence with which the cash is connected.**

Note:

A copy of this application must be given to the person from whom the cash was seized. The justice of the peace who considers this application will require the facts alleged in it to be sworn under oath and may require the applicant to answer any questions under oath. The justice may require any statement in response by the person from whom the cash was seized to be given under oath.

---

*   In the case of a letter, parcel, container or other means of unattended dispatch, insert names, if known, of sender and intended recipient.
** Delete as appropriate.

FORM B

Order for Continued Detention of Seized Cash (Criminal Justice (International Co-operation) Act 1990, s.25(2))

. . . . Magistrates' Court

. . . . Code

Date . . . .

Person from whom money seized . . . . *

Address . . . . *

Amount seized . . . .

Date of seizure . . . .

Time of seizure . . . .

Place of seizure . . . .

On the application of .... (name of applicant), after hearing oral

evidence from the applicant/representations from .... (name),
being the person from whom the cash was seized,

Decision. It is ordered that the above-mentioned cash be further detained for a
period of ....
.... (state period up to a maximum of three months) from the date of this
order or until its release may be sooner directed.

Notice of this order must be given forthwith by the applicant to any person
appearing to him to be affected by it. Such notice shall be in the form set out
overleaf, and shall be accompanied by a copy of this order.

Justice of the Peace

---

*   In the case of a letter, parcel, container or other means of unattended dispatch, insert
    names, if known, of sender and intended recipient.

NOTICE TO PERSONS AFFECTED BY ORDER FOR CONTINUED DETENTION
OF SEIZED CASH

Cash in the sum of .... (amount) was seized on .... (date and

time) .... at (place) from .... (person from

whom seized), and on ..... (date of order) an order was made under section
25(2) of the Criminal Justice (International Co-operation) Act 1990 authorising
the continued detention of the cash for a period of .... (state period).
A copy of the order is enclosed with this notice.

You are being given notice of the order because it appears that you may be
affected by it. You may be able to apply for the release of the cash under section
25(5) of the Criminal Justice (International Co-operation) Act 1990.

At the end of the above-mentioned period of detention an application may be
made for its further detention. You will be notified by the court if such an
application is made, or if any other person makes an application to the court for
release of the cash.

Signed ....
Date ....

FORM C

Application for Further Detention of Seized Cash (Criminal Justice (International Co-operation) Act 1990, s.25(3))

.... Magistrates' Court

.... Code

Date ....

Date of order for continued detention of seized cash ....

(Name of applicant) .... of ....
(address and official position of applicant) applies for an order under section 25(3) of the Criminal Justice (International Co-operation) Act 1990 authorising the further detention of cash in the sum of .... (amount).

To: The Clerk to the Justices

.... Magistrates' Court

FORM D

Direction for Release of Detained Cash (Criminal Justice (International Co-operation) Act 1990, s.25(2))

.... Magistrates' Court

.... Code

Date ....

On the application of (name of applicant) ....

of (address of applicant) ....

after hearing oral evidence from .... /representations from ....

..............................,

Decision. It is directed that the sum of ...., together with the interest accruing thereon in accordance with section 27 of the Criminal Justice (International Co-operation) Act 1990, be released to or to the order of .... (name) on or before .... (date, not more than 7 days from date of order or such later date as with the agreement of the person from whom the cash has been seized may be specified).

Justice of the Peace

FORM E

Application for Forfeiture of Cash Seized Under Section 25 Criminal Justice (International Co-operation) Act 1990 (Criminal Justice (International Co-operation) Act 1990, s.26(1))

.... Magistrates' Court

.... Code

Date ....

(Name of applicant) .... of ....

(address and official position of applicant) applies for an order under section 26(1) of the Criminal Justice (International Co-operation) Act 1990 for the forfeiture of cash in the sum of .... (amount) seized on

(date and time) ....

from .... (person from whom seized), together with any interest accruing thereon pursuant to section 27 of that Act, on the grounds that the said cash

      (i) directly or indirectly represents any person's proceeds of drug trafficking, and/or

      (ii) is intended by any person for use in drug trafficking.*

To: The Clerk to the Justices

.... Magistrates' Court

---

* Delete as appropriate

The Criminal Justice (International Co-operation) Act 1990 (Enforcement Officers) Order 1992

(S.I. No. 77)

Made	*16th January 1992*
Laid before Parliament	*24th January 1992*
Coming into force	*15th February 1992*

In exercise of the powers conferred on me by paragraph 1(1)(c) of Schedule 3 to the Criminal Justice (International Co-operation) Act 1990, and for the purposes of that Schedule, I hereby make the following Order:

1. This Order may be cited as the Criminal Justice (International Co-operation) Act 1990 (Enforcement Officers) Order 1992 and shall come into force on 15th February 1992.

2. The following descriptions of persons, in addition to those specified in paragraph 1(a) and (b) of Schedule 3 to the Criminal Justice (International Co-operation) Act 1990 (enforcement powers in respect of ships), shall be enforcement officers under that Schedule—

    (a) commissioned officers of any of Her Majesty's ships;

    (b) officers of the sea-fishery inspectorate of the Minister of Agriculture, Fisheries and Food;

    (c) officers of the fishery protection service of the Secretary of State for Scotland holding the rank of commander, first officer or second officer.

APPENDIX XXXV

The Controlled Drugs (Substances Useful for Manufacture) Regulations 1991

(S.I. No. 1285)

[These regulations are printed as amended by the Controlled Drugs (Substances Useful for Manufacture) (Amendment) Regulations 1992 (S.I. 1992 No. 2914).]

Made	*30th May 1991*
Laid before Parliament	*7th June 1991*
Coming into force	*1st July 1991*

In exercise of the powers conferred upon me by section 2(2) of the European Communities Act 1972 and by section 13 of the Criminal Justice (International Co-operation) Act 1990, in accordance with regulation 1(2) below, I hereby make the following Regulations:

1.—(1) These Regulations may be cited as the Controlled Drugs (Substances Useful for Manufacture) Regulations 1991 and shall come into force on 1st July 1991.

(2) These Regulations are made under section 2(2) of the 1972 Act and section 13 of the 1990 Act, subject to the following exceptions:

(a) regulations 3 to 6 are made under section 2(2) of the 1972 Act alone; and

(b) regulation 7 is made under section 13 of the 1990 Act alone.

2. In these Regulations:

"the 1972 Act" means the European Communities Act 1972;

"the 1979 Act" means the Customs and Excise Management Act 1979;

"the 1990 Act" means the Criminal Justice (International Co-operation) Act 1990;

"the Community Regulation" means Council Regulation (EEC) No. 3677/90, and "operator" has the same meaning as in that Regulation.

[Article 2a—see Appendix XXXVI, *post*]

3. Subject to regulations 4 and 6 below:

(a) the obligations imposed on operators by Article 2(2) and (3) of the Community Regulation and by virtue of regulation 5 below shall be

119

treated as if they were requirements imposed on them by regulations made under section 13(1) of the 1990 Act;

[The Regulation is set out in Appendix XXXVI, *post*]

4. In Article 4 of the Community Regulation:
(a) the words "the competent authorities of the Member State" shall be taken as a reference to the Secretary of State;

5.—(1) An operator who is concerned in an export, import or transit operation involving a scheduled substance shall ensure that he has the documentation required by Article 2(1) of the Community Regulation.

In this paragraph, "export", "import", "scheduled substance" and "transit" have the same meanings as in the Community Regulation.

(2) The obligations imposed by Article 2(4) of the Community Regulation shall be complied with by the operator mentioned in paragraph (1) of this regulation, and in that Article the words "the competent authorities" shall be taken as a reference to the Secretary of State.

"**5A.**—(1) An operator who is concerned in an export operation involving a scheduled substance in Category 1 of the Annex to the Community Regulation shall ensure that he has the authorisation required by Article 4 of that Regulation.

(2) An operator who is concerned in an export operation involving a scheduled substance in Category 2 of the Annex to the Community Regulation shall ensure that he has such authorisation as is required by Article 5 of that Regulation.

(3) An operator who is concerned in an export operation involving a scheduled substance in Category 3 of the Annex to the Community Regulation shall ensure that he has such authorisation, if any, as is required by Article 5a of that Regulation.

(4) For the purposes of section 68 of the 1979 Act (offences relating to exportation of prohibited or restricted goods) any scheduled substance shall be deemed to be exported contrary to a restriction for the time being in force with respect to it under these Regulations if it is exported without the requisite authorisation having been obtained.

(5) In this regulation, "export" (except where it occurs in paragraph (4) above) and "scheduled substance" have the same meanings as in the Community Regulation, and in Articles 4, 5 and 5a of the Community Regulation the words "the competent authorities" shall be taken as a reference to the Secretary of State.

5B. An operator who fails to comply with any of the requirements imposed by Article 2a of the Community Regulation is guilty of an offence and liable:
(a) on summary conviction, to imprisonment for a term not exceeding 3 months or a fine not exceeding the statutory maximum or both;
(b) on conviction on indictment, to imprisonment for a term not exceeding two years or a fine or both.

5C.—(1) An operator who fails to comply with any of the requirements imposed by virtue of regulation 5A above is guilty of an offence and liable to the same penalties as an operator who is guilty of an offence under regulation 5B above.

(2) The powers conferred by subsection (1) of section 23 of the Misuse of Drugs Act 1971 shall be exercisable also for the purposes of the execution of

Articles 4, 5 and 5a of the Community Regulation and subsection (3) of that section (excluding paragraph (a)) shall apply also to the offence under paragraph (1) above, taking references in those subsections to controlled drugs as references to scheduled substances within the meaning of the Community Regulation.

5D. Any reference in regulations 5B and 5C above to an operator who fails to comply with the requirements mentioned in those regulations shall include an operator who, in purported compliance with any such requirement:

    (a) furnishes information which he knows to be false in a material particular; or

    (b) recklessly furnishes information which is false in a material particular.".

6. Where a person is convicted of an offence contrary to section 68 of the 1979 Act or section 13(5) of the 1990 Act as a result of the application of regulation 3 above:

    (a) section 68(1) of the 1979 Act shall have effect as if after the word "greater" there were added the words "but not exceeding the statutory maximum";

    (b) section 68(3)(a) of the 1979 Act shall have effect as if after the word "greater" there were added the words "but not exceeding the statutory maximum", and for the words "6 months" there were substituted the words "3 months";

    (c) section 68(3)(b) of the 1979 Act shall have effect as if for the words "7 years" there were substituted the words "2 years";

    (d) section 13(5)(a) of the 1990 Act shall have effect as if for the words "6 months" there were substituted the words "3 months".

7. A person who produces or supplies a scheduled substance specified in Table 1 in Schedule 2 to the 1990 Act shall:

    (a) make a record of each quantity of such scheduled substance produced or supplied by him, as the case may be; and

    (b) preserve all records made under this regulation for a period of not less than two years from the end of the calendar year in which the production or supply, as the case may be, took place.

In this regulation, "produce" and "supply" have the same meanings as in the Misuse of Drugs Act 1971.

Regulation (EEC) 3677/90 as amended by Regulation (EEC) 900/92

TITLE I

GENERAL

ARTICLE 1

1. This Regulation lays down the measures to be taken to monitor trade between the Community and third countries in substances frequently used for the illicit manufacture of narcotic drugs and psychotropic substances for the purpose of preventing the diversion of such substances.

2. For the purposes of this Regulation:

(a) "scheduled substance" means any substance listed in the Annex, including mixtures containing such substances. This excludes pharmaceutical preparations or other preparations containing schedule substances that are compounded in such a way that such substances cannot be easily used or recovered by readily applicable means;

(b) "import" means any physical introduction of scheduled substances into the customs territory of the Community;

(c) "export" means any physical departure of scheduled substances from the customs territory of the Community which requires a customs export declaration;

(d) "transit" means any transport of scheduled substances between third countries through the customs territory of the Community and any transhipment in that territory;

(e) "operator" means any natural or legal person engaged in the manufacture, production, trade or distribution of scheduled substances in the Community or involved in other related activities such as import, export, transit, broking and processing of scheduled substances. This definition includes, in particular, persons pursuing the activity of making customs declarations on a self-employed basis, either as their principal occupation or as a secondary activity related to another occupation;

(f) "ultimate consignee" means any natural or legal person to which the scheduled substances are delivered in the country of destination. This person may be different from the end-user."[1]

(g) "International Narcotics Control Board" means the Board established

1 Inserted by reg. 900/92.

by the Single Convention on Narcotic Drugs, 1961, as amended by the 1972 Protocol.

TITLE II

MONITORING OF TRADE

ARTICLE 2

Documentation, records and labelling

The import, export and transit of scheduled substances are subject to the following requirements:

1. All import, export and transit operations shall be properly documented. In particular, commercial documents such as invoices, cargo manifests, customs, transport and other shipping documents shall contain sufficient information positively to identify:

— the name of the scheduled substance as given in the Annex
— the quantity and weight of the scheduled substance and, where it consists of a mixture, the quantity and weight of the mixture as well as the quantity and weight or the percentage of any substance or substances listed in the Annex which are contained in the mixture,[2]
— the name and address of the exporter, the importer, the distributor and, in accordance with Articles 4, 5 and 5a, the ultimate consignee.[3]

2. Where operators affix labels indicating the type of product or its trade name to scheduled substances in import, export or transit operations, such labels must show the names of the substances as given in the Annex.
3. Operators involved in import, export and transit of scheduled substances shall keep detailed records of those activities.
4. The document and records referred to in points 1 and 3 shall be kept for a period of three years from the end of the calendar year in which the operation referred to in point 1 took place, and must be readily available for inspection by the competent authorities upon request.[4]

ARTICLE 2a[5]

Licensing and registration of operators

1. Operators, other than customs agents, warehouse depositors and transporters when acting solely in that capacity, engaged in the import, export or transit of scheduled substances listed in Category 1 of the Annex shall be required to obtain a licence from the Member State in which they are established to qualify for this activity. In considering whether to grant a licence, the competent authority shall take into account the competence and integrity of the applicant.

The licence may be suspended or revoked by the competent authorities whenever there are reasonable grounds for belief that the holder is no longer a fit

---

2 Substituted by reg. 900/92.
3 Inserted by reg. 900/92.
4 Substituted by reg. 900/92.
5 Inserted by reg. 900/92.

and proper person to hold a licence, or that the conditions under which the licence was issued are no longer fulfilled.

2. Operators, other than customs agents, warehouse depositors and transporters when acting solely in that capacity, engaged in the import, export or transit of scheduled substances listed in Category 2 or the export of scheduled substances listed in Category 3 of the Annex are required to register and update with the competent authorities the addresses of the premises from which they manufacture or trade in these substances.

However, this requirement shall not apply in respect of operators engaged in the export of small quantities of scheduled substances listed in Category 3 or the export of mixtures containing scheduled substances listed in Category 3 which have been identified to that end.

3. The Member States shall determine the procedures for issuing licences, including the attachment of specific conditions, such as the length of their validity and the charging of fees for their issue.

ARTICLE 3[6]

Co-operation

The Member States shall take the necessary measures to establish close co-operation between the competent authorities and operations, so that operators:

— notify the competent authorities immediately of any circumstances, such as unusual orders and transactions involving scheduled substances, with suggest that such substances intended for import, export or transit may be diverted for the illicit manufacture of narcotic drugs of psychotrophic substances,

— provide the competent authorities in summary form such information about their export transactions as the competent authorities may require.

ARTICLE 4

Export authorization[7]

Scheduled substances listed in Category 1 of the Annex

1. The exportation of scheduled substances listed in Category 1 of the Annex shall be subject to authorization in the form of individual export authorizations issued by the competent authorities of the Member State in which the customs export declaration is to be lodged in accordance with the provisions in force.

2. Applications for authorizations referred to in paragraph 1 shall contain the following information:

— the name and address of the exporter, the importer in the third country and any other operator involved in the export operation or shipment, and also of the ultimate consignee,

— the name of the scheduled substances as given in Category 1 in the Annex,

6 Substituted by reg. 900/92.
7 Substituted by reg. 900/92.

— the quantity and weight of the scheduled substance and, where it consists of a mixture, the quantity and weight of the mixture as well as the quantity and weight or the percentage of any substance or substances listed in the Annex which are contained in the mixture,

— details as to the transport arrangements, and in particular the expected date of dispatch, method of transport, name of the customs office where the customs export declaration is to be lodged, and, in so far as such information is available at this stage, identification of the means of transport, itinerary, expected point of exit from Community customs territory and the point of entry into the importing country.

In the case of paragraph 10, a copy of the import permit issued by the destination country must be attached to the application.

3. A decision on the application shall be taken within a period of 15 working days from the date on which the competent authority considers the file to be complete. This period shall be extended if, in the case of paragraph 10, the authorities are obliged to make further enquiries in order to satisfy themselves that the importation of the substances has been properly authorized.

4. Without prejudice to any possible implementation of technical enforcement measures, the export authorization referred to in paragraph 1 shall be refused, if:

(a) there are reasonable grounds to suspect that the information supplied in compliance with the obligations under paragraph 2 is false or incorrect;

(b) in the case of paragraph 10, it is established that the importation of the scheduled substances has not been properly authorized by the competent authorities of the country of destination;

(c) there are reasonable grounds for suspecting that the substances in question are intended for the illicit manufacture of narcotic drugs or psychotropic substances.

5. If the particulars on the itinery and means of transport were not contained in the application referred to in paragraph 2, the export authorization shall state that the operator must furnish these particulars to the customs or other competent authority at the point of exit from the Community customs territory before the physical departure of the consignment. In this case, the export authorization shall be annotated accordingly at the time of issue.

6. In all cases, the export authorization shall be produced for inspection by the customs authorities when the customs export declaration is lodged.

A copy of this authorization shall furthermore accompany the consignment until the customs office at the point of exit of the scheduled substances from the Community customs territory. The office shall insert, where appropriate, the particulars referred to in paragraph 5 and any other necessary particulars and apply its stamp to the copy of the authorization before returning it to the issuing authority.

7. The issue of an export authorization does not preclude any possible administrative or other liability of the holder of such authorization.

8. The export authorization may be suspended or revoked by the competent authorities whenever there are reasonable grounds to suspect that the substances might be diverted to the illicit manufacture of narcotic drugs or psychotropic substances.

9. With regard to requests for pre-export notification addressed to the Community by a third country pursuant to Article 12(10) of the United Nations Convention:

(a) the Commission shall immediately communicate to the competent authorities of the Member States any such request received;

(b) the competent authorities of the Member State concerned shall, prior to any export of scheduled substances to the requesting country, supply the information specified in paragraph 2 to the competent authorities of that country. A copy of this reply shall be communicated to the Commission for circulation to the other Member States;

(c) the authority furnishing such information shall require that the authority in the third country receiving the information shall keep confidential any trade, business, commercial or professional secret or any trade process referred to therein.

10. Whenever there is agreement between the Community and a third country that exports shall not be authorized unless an import permit has been issued by the competent authorities of the latter country for the substances in question:

(a) the Commission shall communicate to the competent authorities in the Member States the name and address of the competent authority in the third country together with any operational information obtained from this country;

(b) the competent authorities in the Member States shall satisfy themselves that any importation has been properly authorized, if necessary, by requesting confirmation from the authority referred to under point (a).

ARTICLE 5[8]

Specific export requirements

Scheduled substances listed in Category 2 of the Annex

1. The exportation of scheduled substances listed in Category 2 of the Annex shall be subject to an authorization issued in accordance with paragraphs 2 and 3 by the competent authorities of the Member State in which the customs export declaration is to be lodged in accordance with the provisions in force.

2. Exports referred to in paragraph 1 shall be subject *mutatis mutandis* to the provisions of Article 4, wherever they appear to be intended, directly or indirectly, for any third country which has been identified to be concerned by the illicit manufacture of those narcotic drugs or psychotropic substances by the use of the scheduled substances in question. The said identification shall be based, in particular, on a reasoned request to the Commission by the third country concerned.

The provisions of Article 4 shall also apply whenever an open individual authorization cannot be issued under paragraph 3.

3. In all other cases, the exportation of scheduled substances listed in Category 2 may be authorized at the request of the operators concerned on a global basis by the issue of an open individual authorization. The decision to issue such an authorization shall take into account the competence and integrity of the applicant together with the nature, volume and pattern of his involvement in these substances. In such cases, the holder shall enter the details of this authorization in the relevant customs export declaration.

In accordance with the provisions laid down by the competent authorities, the holder of such an authorization shall furnish information in a summary form about exports made under the authority of the authorization.

8 Substituted by reg. 900/92.

The open individual authorization may be suspended or revoked whenever there are reasonable grounds for belief that its holder is no longer a fit and proper person to hold an authorization, or that the conditions under which the authorization was issued are no longer valid.

ARTICLE 5a[9]

Specific export requirements

Scheduled substances listed in Category 3 of the Annex

1. Wherever the export of scheduled substances listed in Category 3 of the Annex is intended, directly or indirectly, for any third country:

(a) with which the Community has concluded an agreement whereby no export from the Community to that country shall be authorized unless the competent authorities of the country have issued an import permit in respect of the consignment in question; or

(b) which has been identified as a country concerned by the illicit manufacture of heroin or cocaine on its territory or as a sensitive country as regards the possible diversion of the said substances,

such export shall be subject to an authorization issued in accordance with paragraphs 2 and 3 by the competent authorities of the Member State in which the customs export declaration is to be lodged in accordance with the provisions in force.

Exports of substances referred to in paragraph 1 shall be subject *mutatis mutandis* to the provisions of Article 4, wherever, subject to specific arrangements taken between the Community and the countries referred to in paragraph 1, individual export authorization is required. The provisions of Article 4 shall also apply whenever an open individual authorization cannot be issued in accordance with paragraph 3.

3. In appropriate circumstances, the exportation of substances in Category 3 may be authorized on a global basis by the issue of an open individual authorization. The decision to issue, suspend or revoke such authorizations shall be taken by the application *mutatis mutandis* of Article 5(3).

In addition it shall be a condition of the issue of such authorizations that, for control purposes, the holder shall retain for inspection by the competent authorities of the Member State from which the export has taken place, where appropriate and in respect of each export, a copy of the import permit issued by the authorities of the third country. In cases of doubt, the competent authorities of the Member States of exportation may contact the authorities which have issued the import permit.

TITLE III

CONTROL MEASURES

ARTICLE 6[10]

Powers of competent authorities

1. In order to ensure the correct application of Articles 2, 4, 5 and 5a, each

9 Inserted by reg. 900/92.
10 Substituted by reg. 900/92.

Member State shall adopt within the framework of its domestic law the measures necessary to enable the competent authorities.

(a) to obtain information on any orders for or operations involving scheduled substances;

(b) to enter operators' business premises in order to obtain evidence of irregularities.

2. Without prejudice to the measures laid down in Articles 4, 5 and 5a and paragraph 1 of this Article the competent authorities of each Member State may prohibit the introduction of scheduled substances into Community customs territory or their departure from it, if there are reasonable grounds for suspecting that the substances are intended for the illicit manufacture of narcotic drugs or psychotropic substances.

3. For the purpose of preventing specific risks of diversion in free zones as well as in other sensitive areas such as bonded warehouses, Member States shall ensure that controls applied to operations carried out in these areas are effective at every stage of these operations and not less stringent than those applied in the other parts of the customs territory.

TITLE IV

ADMINISTRATIVE CO-OPERATION

ARTICLE 7

For the purposes of applying this Regulation and without prejudice to Article 10, the provisions of Regulation (EEC) No. 1468/81 and in particular those on confidentiality shall apply *mutatis mutandis*. Each Member State shall communicate to the other Member States and to the Commission the name of the competent authorities appointed to act as correspondents in accordance with Article 2(2) of Regulation (EEC) No. 1468/81.

TITLE V

FINAL PROVISIONS

ARTICLE 8

Each Member State shall determine the penalties to be applied for infringement of the provisions of this Regulation. The penalties shall be sufficient to promote compliance with those provisions.

ARTICLE 9

1. To permit any necessary adjustments to the arrangements for monitoring trade in scheduled substances between the Community and third countries, the competent authorities in each Member State shall each year communicate to the Commission all relevant information on the implementation of the monitoring measures laid down in this Regulation, in particular as regards substances used for the illicit manufacture of narcotic drugs or psychotropic substances and methods of diversion and illicit manufacture.

2. On the basis of the communications made pursuant to paragraph 1, the Commission shall, pursuant to Article 12(12) of the United Nations Convention and in consultation with the Member States, draw up an annual report to be submitted to the International Narcotics Control Board.

ARTICLE 10[11]

1. The Commission shall be assisted by a committee composed of the representative of the Commission.

The committee shall examine any matter concerning the implementation of this Regulation raised by its chairman either on his own initiative or at the request of a representative of a Member State.

2. The representative of the Commission shall submit to the committee a draft of the measures to be taken. The committee shall deliver its opinion on the draft, within a time limit which the chairman may lay down according to the urgency of the matter. The opinion shall be delivered by the majority laid down in Article 148(2) of the Treaty in the case of decisions which the Council is required to adopt on a proposal from the Commission. The votes of the Member States within the committee shall be weighted in the manner set out in that Article; the Chairman shall not vote.

The commission shall adopt measures which shall apply immediately. However, if these measures are not in accordance with the opinion of the committee, they shall be communicated by the Commission to the Council forthwith. In that event the Commission shall defer application of the measures which it has decided for three months from the date of communication.

The Council, acting by a qualified majority, may take a different decision within the time period referred to in the previous subparagraph.

3. The procedure laid down in paragraph 2 shall be followed in particular for:
  (a) the determination of the quantities of the scheduled substances listed in Category 3 and the identification of mixtures containing scheduled substances listed in Category 3 pursuant to the second subparagraph of Article 2a(2);
  (b) the identification of countries and substances pursuant to Article 5(2);
  (c) the adoption of export authorisation requirements pursuant to paragraph 1(b) of Article 5a whenever there is no agreement with the third country in question;
  (d) the adoption of the model export authorisation form referred to in Article 4 as well as the detailed rules concerning its use and the detailed rules for implementation of the open individual authorisation system referred to in Articles 5 and 5a;
  (e) the amendment of the Annex to this Regulation, in cases where the Annexes to the United National Convention are amended.

11 Substituted by reg. 900/92.

ARTICLE 11

Each Member State shall inform the Commission of the measures it takes pursuant to this Regulation.

The Commission shall communicate this information to the other Member States.

ARTICLE 11a[12]

The Commission is hereby authorised to adopt a position, on behalf of the Community, in favour of amendments to Tables I and II of the Annex to the United Nations Convention which conform to the Annex of this Regulation.

ANNEX C[13]

Substance	CN derivation (if different)	CN code
CATEGORY 1		
— Ephedrine		2939 40 10
— Ergometrine		2939 60 10
— Ergotamine		2939 60 30
— Lysergic acid		2939 60 50
— 1-phenyl-2-propanone	Phenylacetone	2914 30 10
— Pseudoephedrine		2939 40 30
— Acetylanthranilic acid	2-Acetamidobenzoic acid	2924 29 50
— 3,4 Methylenediosyphenyl-propan-2-one		2932 90 77

The salts of the substances listed in this Category whenever the existence of such salts is possible.

---

12 Inserted by reg. 900/92.
13 Under powers provided by Article 10(3)(e) and following a decision taken by the UN Commission on Narcotic Drugs, the Commission implementing Regulation currently propose that these substances be transferred from Category 2 to Category 1.

Substance	CN derivation (if different)	CN code

CATEGORY 2

— Acetic anhydride		2915 24 00
— Anthranilic acid		ex 2922 49 90
— Phenylacetic acid		2916 33 00
— Piperidine		2933 39 30
— Isosafrole (cis + trans)		2932 90 73
— Piperonal		2932 90 75
— Safrole		2932 90 71

The salts of the substances listed in this Category whenever the existence of such salts is possible.

CATEGORY 3

— Acetone		2914 11 00
— Ethyl ether	Diethyl ether	2909 11 00
— Methylethyl ketone (MEK)	Butanone	2914 12 00
— Toluene		2902 30 10/90
— Potassium permanganate		2841 60 10
— Sulphuric acid		2807 00 10
— Hydrochloric acid	Hydrogen chloride	2806 10 00

Article 2 [of 900/92]

This Regulation shall enter into force on the third day following its publication in the *Official Journal of the European Communities*.

It shall apply from 1 January 1993, with the exception of Article 1(11) which shall apply from the date of entry into force of this Regulation [1 July 1991].

This Regulation shall be binding in its entirety and directly applicable in all Member States.

APPENDIX XXXVII

Criminal Justice Act 1993

CHAPTER 36

ARRANGEMENT OF SECTIONS

PART II

DRUG TRAFFICKING OFFENCES

Confiscation orders

132

PART III

PROCEEDS OF CRIMINAL CONDUCT

Confiscation orders

Money laundering and other offences

PART VI

SUPPLEMENTARY

PART II

DRUG TRAFFICKING OFFENCES

Confiscation orders

Confiscation orders

7.—(1) In section 1 of the Drug Trafficking Offences Act 1986 (confiscation orders), in subsection (1), for "the court" there shall be substituted "then—
    (a) if the prosecutor asks it to proceed under this section, or
    (b) if the court considers that, even though the prosecutor has not asked it to do so, it is appropriate for it to proceed under this section,
  it".

(2) After subsection (7) of that section there shall be inserted—
    "(7A) The standard of proof required to determine any question arising under this Act as to—
      (a) whether a person has benefited from drug trafficking, or
      (b) the amount to be recovered in his case by virtue of this section,
  shall be that applicable in civil proceedings."

(3) In subsection (3) of section 4 of the Act of 1986 (amount to be recovered under confiscation order), for the words from "the amount appearing" to the end there shall be substituted "—
    (a) the amount appearing to the court to be the amount that might be so realised, or

(b) a nominal amount, where it appears to the court (on the information available to it at the time) that the amount that might be so realised is nil".

Postponed determinations

8. The following section shall be inserted in the Drug Trafficking Offences Act 1986, after section 1—

"Postponed determinations

1A.—(1) Where the Crown Court is acting under section 1 of this Act but considers that it requires further information before—
  (a) determining whether the defendant has benefited from drug trafficking, or
  (b) determining the amount to be recovered in his case by virtue of section 1 of this Act,
it may, for the purpose of enabling that information to be obtained, postpone making the determination for such period as it may specify.

(2) More than one postponement may be made under subsection (1) above in relation to the same case.

(3) Unless it is satisfied that there are exceptional circumstances, the court shall not specify a period under subsection (1) above which—
  (a) by itself, or
  (b) where there has been one or more previous postponements under subsection (1) above or (4) below, when taken together with the earlier specified period or periods,
exceeds six months beginning with the date of conviction.

(4) Where the defendant appeals against his conviction, the court may, on that account—
  (a) postpone making either or both of the determinations mentioned in subsection (1) above for such period as it may specify, or
  (b) where it has already exercised its powers under this section to postpone, extend the specified period.

(5) A postponement or extension under subsection (1) or (4) above may be made—
  (a) on application by the defendant or the prosecutor, or
  (b) by the court of its own motion.

(6) Unless the court is satisfied that there are exceptional circumstances any postponement or extension under subsection (4) above shall not exceed the period ending three months after the date on which the appeal is determined or otherwise disposed of.

(7) Where the court exercises its power under subsection (1) or (4) above, it may nevertheless proceed to sentence, or otherwise deal with, the defendant in respect of the relevant offence or any of the relevant offences.

(8) Where the court has so proceeded, section 1 of this Act shall have effect as if—
  (a) in subsection (4), the words from "before sentencing" to "offences concerned" were omitted, and
  (b) in subsection (5)(c), after "determining" there were inserted "in relation to any offence in respect of which he has not been sentenced or otherwise dealt with".

(9) In sentencing, or otherwise dealing with, the defendant in respect of the relevant offence or any of the relevant offences at any time during the specified period, the court shall not—
  (a) impose any fine on him, or
  (b) make any such order as is mentioned in section 1(5)(b)(ii) or (iii) of this Act.
(10) In this section—
  (a) "the relevant offence" means the drug trafficking offence in respect of which the defendant appears (as mentioned in section 1(1) of this Act) before the court;
  (b) references to an appeal include references to an application under section 111 of the Magistrates' Courts Act 1980 (statement of case by magistrates' court)."
(11) In this section "the date of conviction" means—
  (a) the date on which the defendant was convicted, or
  (b) where he appeared to be sentenced in respect of more than one conviction, and those convictions were not all on the same date, the date of the latest of those convictions.".

Assumptions about proceeds of drug trafficking

9.—(1) Section 2 of the Drug Trafficking Offences Act 1986 (assessing proceeds of drug trafficking) shall be amended as follows.
(2) In subsection (2)—
  (a) for "may" there shall be substituted "shall"; and
  (b) for the words from "following" to the end there shall be substituted "required assumptions".
(3) After subsection (2), there shall be inserted—
  "(2A) The court shall not make any required assumption if—
    (a) that assumption is shown to be incorrect in the defendant's case, or
    (b) the court is satisfied that there would be a serious risk of injustice in his case if the assumption were to be made.
  (2B) Where the court does not apply one or more of the required assumptions it shall state its reasons.".
(4) In subsection (3)—
  (a) for "Those" there shall be substituted "The required"; and
  (b) in paragraph (a)(i), for "him" there shall be substituted "the defendant".

Provision of information

10.—(1) Section 3 of the Drug Trafficking Offences Act 1986 (statements relating to drug trafficking) shall be amended in accordance with subsections (2) to (4).
(2) For subsections (1) and (2), there shall be substituted—
  "(1) Where the prosecutor asks the court to proceed under section 1 of this Act or applies to the court under section 4A, 5A, 5B or 5C of this Act he shall give the court, within such period as it may direct, a statement of matters which he considers relevant in connection with—
    (a) determining whether the defendant has benefited from drug trafficking, or
    (b) assessing the value of his proceeds of drug trafficking.

(1A) In this section such a statement is referred to as a "prosecutor's statement".

(1B) Where the court proceeds under section 1 of this Act without the prosecutor having asked it to do so, it may require him to give it a prosecutor's statement, within such period as it may direct.

(1C) Where the prosecutor has given a prosecutor's statement—
    (a) he may at any time give the court a further such statement, and
    (b) the court may at any time require him to give it a further such statement, within such period as it may direct.

(1D) Where any prosecutor's statement has been given and the court is satisfied that a copy of the statement has been served on the defendant, it may require the defendant—
    (a) to indicate to it, within such period as it may direct, the extent to which he accepts each allegation in the statement, and
    (b) so far as he does not accept any such allegation, to give particulars of any matters on which he proposes to rely.

(1E) Where the court has given a direction under this section it may at any time vary it by giving a further direction.

(2) Where the defendant accepts to any extent any allegation in any prosecutor's statement, the court may, for the purposes of—
    (a) determining whether the defendant has benefited from drug trafficking, or
    (b) assessing the value of his proceeds of drug trafficking,
treat his acceptance as conclusive of the matters to which it relates."

(3) In subsection (3), for "statement" there shall be substituted "prosecutor's statement in question".

(4) For subsection (5) there shall be substituted—

"(5) An allegation may be accepted, or particulars of any matter may be given, for the purposes of this section in such manner as the court may direct."

(5) The following section shall be inserted in the Act of 1986, after section 3—

"Provision of information by defendant

3A.—(1) This section applies where—
    (a) the prosecutor has asked the court to proceed under section 1 of this Act or has applied to the court under section 5A, 5B or 5C of this Act, or
    (b) no such request has been made but the court is nevertheless proceeding, or considering whether to proceed, under section 1.

(2) For the purpose of obtaining information to assist it in carrying out its functions, the court may at any time order the defendant to give it such information as may be specified in the order.

(3) An order under subsection (2) above may require all, or any specified part, of the required information to be given to the court in such manner, and before such date, as may be specified in the order.

(4) Crown Court Rules may make provision as to the maximum or minimum period that may be allowed under subsection (3) above.

(5) If the defendant fails, without reasonable excuse, to comply with any order under this section, the court may draw such inference from that failure as it considers appropriate.

(6) Where the prosecutor accepts to any extent any allegation made by the

defendant in giving to the court information required by an order under this section, the court may treat that acceptance as conclusive of the matters to which it relates.

(7) For the purposes of this section, an allegation may be accepted in such manner as the court may direct.".

(6) In section 5(3) of the Act of 1986 the words "sections 3 and 4 of" shall be omitted.

Variation of confiscation orders

11.—(1) Section 14 of the Drug Trafficking Offences Act 1986 (variation of confiscation orders) shall be amended as follows.

(2) In subsection (1) (variation on application of defendant), after "defendant" there shall be inserted "or a receiver appointed under section 8 or 11 of this Act, or in pursuance of a charging order, made".

(3) In subsection (3), for "defendant" there shall be substituted "person who applied for it".

(4) The following shall be inserted at the end—
"(5) Rules of court may make provision—
   (a) for the giving of notice of any application under this section; and
   (b) for any person appearing to the court to be likely to be affected by any exercise of its powers under this section to be given an opportunity to make representations to the court.".

Revised assessment of proceeds of drug trafficking

12. The following section shall be inserted in the Drug Trafficking Offences Act 1986, after section 5—

"Reconsideration of case where court has not proceeded under section 1"

5A.—(1) This section applies where the defendant has appeared before the Crown Court to be sentenced in respect of one or more drug trafficking offences but the court has not proceeded under section 1 of this Act.

(2) If the prosecutor has evidence—
   (a) which was not available to him when the defendant appeared to be sentenced (and accordingly was not considered by the court), but
   (b) which the prosecutor believes would have led the court to determine that the defendant had benefited from drug trafficking if—
      (i) the prosecutor had asked the court to proceed under section 1 of this Act, and
      (ii) the evidence had been considered by the court,
he may apply to the Crown Court for it to consider the evidence.

(3) The court shall proceed under section 1 of this Act if, having considered the evidence, it is satisfied that it is appropriate to do so.

(4) In considering whether it is appropriate to proceed under section 1, the court shall have regard to all the circumstances of the case.

(5) Where, having decided to proceed under section 1, the court proposes to make a confiscation order against the defendant, it shall order the payment of such amount as it thinks just in all the circumstances of the case.

(6) In considering the circumstances of any case the court shall have

regard, in particular, to the amount of any fine imposed on the defendant in respect of the offence or offences in question.

(7) Where the court is proceeding under section 1 of this Act, by virtue of this section, subsection (4) of that section shall have effect as if the words "before sentencing or otherwise dealing with him in respect of the offence or, as the case may be, any of the offences concerned" were omitted.

(8) The court may take into account any payment or other reward received by the defendant on or after the date of conviction, but only if the prosecutor shows that it was received by the defendant in connection with drug trafficking carried on by the defendant or another on or before that date.

(9) In considering any evidence under this section which relates to any payment or reward to which subsection (8) above applies, the court shall not make the assumptions which would otherwise be required by section 2 of this Act.

(10) No application shall be entertained by the court under this section if it is made after the end of the period of six years beginning with the date of conviction.

(11) In this section "the date of conviction" means—
    (a) the date on which the defendant was convicted, or
    (b) where he appears to be sentenced in respect of more than one conviction, and those convictions were not all on the same date, the date of the latest of those convictions.

Reassessment of whether defendant has benefited from drug trafficking

5B.—(1) This section applies where the court has made a determination ("the section 1(2) determination") under section 1(2) of this Act that the defendant has not benefited from drug trafficking.

(2) If the prosecutor has evidence—
    (a) which was not considered by the court in making the section 1(2) determination, but
    (b) which the prosectuor believes would have led the court to determine that the defendant had benefited from drug trafficking if it had been considered by the court,
he may apply to the Crown Court for it to consider that evidence.

(3) If, having considered the evidence, the court is satisfied that it would have determined that the defendant had benefited from drug trafficking if that evidence had been available to it, the court—
    (a) shall—
        (i) make a fresh determination under subsection (2) of section 1 of this Act; and
        (ii) make a determination under subsection (4) of that section of the amount to be recovered by virtue of that section; and
    (b) may make an order under that section.

(4) Where the court is proceeding under section 1 of this Act, by virtue of this section, subsection (4) of that section shall have effect as if the words "before sentencing or otherwise dealing with him in respect of the offence or, as the case may be, any of the offences concerned" were omitted.

(5) The court may take into account any payment or other reward received by the defendant on or after the date of the section 1(2) determination, but only if the prosecutor shows that it was received by the defendant in

connection with drug trafficking carried on by the defendant or another on or before that date.

(6) In considering any evidence under this section which relates to any payment or reward to which subsection (5) applies, the court shall not make the assumptions which would otherwise be required by section 2 of this Act.

(7) Where the High Court—

    (a) has been asked to proceed under section 4A of this Act in relation to a defendant who has absconded, but

    (b) has decided not to make a confiscation order against him,

this section shall not apply at any time while he remains an absconder.

(8) No application shall be entertained by the court under this section if it is made after the end of the period of six years beginning with—

    (a) the date on which the defendant was convicted;
    or

    (b) where he appeared to be sentenced in respect of more than one conviction, and those convictions were not all on the same date, the date of the latest of those convictions.

Revised assessment of proceeds of drug trafficking

5C.—(1) This section applies where the court has made a determination under section 1(4) of this Act of the amount to be recovered in a particular case by virtue of that section ("the current section 1(4) determination").

(2) Where the prosecutor is of the opinion that the real value of the defendant's proceeds of drug trafficking was greater than their assessed value, the prosecutor may apply to the Crown Court for the evidence on which the prosecutor has formed his opinion to be considered by the court.

(3) In subsection (2) above—

    "assessed value" means the value of the defendant's proceeds of drug trafficking as assessed by the court under section 4(1) of this Act; and

    "real value" means the value of the defendant's proceeds of drug trafficking which took place—

        (a) in the period by reference to which the current section 1(4) determination was made;
        or
        (b) in any earlier period.

(4) If, having considered the evidence, the court is satisfied that the real value of the defendant's proceeds of drug trafficking is greater than their assessed value (whether because the real value was higher at the time of the current section 1(4) determination than was thought or because the value of the proceeds in question has subsequently increased), the court shall make a fresh determination under subsection (4) of section 1 of this Act of the amount to be recovered by virtue of that section.

(5) Where the court is proceeding under section 1 of this Act, by virtue of this section, subsection (4) of that section shall have effect as if the words "before sentencing or otherwise dealing with him in respect of the offence or, as the case may be, any of the offences concerned" were omitted.

(6) Any determination under section 1(4) of this Act by virtue of this section shall be by reference to the amount that might be realised at the time when the determination is made.

(7) For any determination under section 1(4) of this Act by virtue of this

section, section 2(5) of this Act shall not apply in relation to any of the defendant's proceeds of drug trafficking taken into account in respect of the current section 1(4) determination.

(8) In relation to any such determination—

    (a) sections 3(4)(a), 4(2) and 5(7) of this Act shall have effect as if for "confiscation order" there were substituted "determination";

    (b) section 4(3) of this Act shall have effect as if for "confiscation order is made" there were substituted "determination is made"; and

    (c) section 5(3) of this Act shall have effect as if for "a confiscation order is made against the defendant" there were substituted "of the determination".

(9) The court may take into account any payment or other reward received by the defendant on or after the date of the current section 1(4) determination, but only if the prosecutor shows that it was received by the defendant in connection with drug trafficking carried on by the defendant or another on or before that date.

(10) In considering any evidence under this section which relates to any payment or reward to which subsection (9) above applies, the court shall not make the assumptions which would otherwise be required by section 2 of this Act.

(11) If, as a result of making the fresh determination required by subsection (4) above, the amount to be recovered exceeds the amount set by the current section 1(4) determination, the court may substitute for the amount to be recovered under the confiscation order which was made by reference to the current section 1(4) determination such greater amount as it thinks just in all the circumstances of the case.

(12) Where the court varies a confiscation order under subsection (11) above, it shall substitute for the term of imprisonment or of detention fixed under section 31(2) of the Powers of Criminal Courts Act 1973 in respect of the amount to be recovered under the order a longer term determined in accordance with that section (as it has effect by virtue of section 6 of this Act) in respect of the greater amount substituted under subsection (11) above.

(13) Subsection (12) above shall apply only if the effect of the substitution is to increase the maximum period applicable in relation to the order under section 31(3A) of the Act of 1973.

(14) Where a confiscation order has been made in relation to any defendant by virtue of section 4A of this Act, this section shall not apply at any time while he is an absconder.

(15) No application shall be entertained by the court under this section if it is made after the end of the period of six years beginning with—

    (a) the date on which the defendant was convicted;
    or

    (b) where he appeared to be sentenced in respect of more than one conviction, and those convictions were not all on the same date, the date of the latest of those convictions.".

Availability of powers and satisfaction of orders

13.—(1) In section 6 of the Drug Trafficking Offences Act 1986 (default in complying with confiscation order: application of procedure for enforcing fines), the following subsection shall be added at the end—

    "(7) Where the defendant serves a term of imprisonment or detention in default of paying any amount due under a confiscation order, his serving that term does not prevent the confiscation order from continuing to have effect, so far as any other method of enforcement is concerned.".

(2) Section 7 of the Act of 1986 (cases in which restraint orders and charging orders may be made) shall be amended as set out in subsections (3) to (5).

(3) The following subsection shall be substituted for subsection (1)—

"(1) The powers conferred on the High Court by sections 8(1) and 9(1) of this Act are exercisable where—

    (a) proceedings have been instituted in England and Wales against the defendant for a drug trafficking offence or an application has been made by the prosecutor in respect of the defendant under section 16 of the Criminal Justice (International Co-operation) Act 1990 (increase in realisable property) or section 4A, 5A, 5B or 5C of this Act,

    (b) the proceedings have not, or the application has not, been concluded, and

    (c) the court is satisfied that there is reasonable cause to believe—

        (i) in the case of an application under section 5C of this Act or section 16 of the Act of 1990, that the court will be satisfied as mentioned in section 5C(4) of this Act or, as the case may be, section 16(2) of the Act of 1990, or

        (ii) in any other case, that the defendant has benefited from drug trafficking.".

(4) The following subsection shall be substituted for subsection (2)—

"(2) Those powers are also exercisable where—

    (a) the court is satisfied that, whether by the laying of an information or otherwise, a person is to be charged with a drug trafficking offence or that an application of a kind mentioned in subsection (1)(a) above is to be made in respect of the defendant, and

    (b) the court is also satisfied as mentioned in subsection (1)(c) above.".

(5) The following subsections shall be added at the end—

"(5) Where the court has made an order under section 8(1) or 9(1) of this Act in relation to a proposed application by virtue of subsection (2) above, the court shall discharge the order if the application is not made within such time as the court considers reasonable.

(6) The court shall not exercise powers under section 8(1) or 9(1) of this Act, by virtue of subsection (1) above, if it is satisfied that—

    (a) there has been undue delay in continuing the proceedings or application in question; or

    (b) the prosecutor does not intend to proceed.".

(6) In section 8 of the Act of 1986 (restraint orders), the following subsection shall be substituted for subsection (5)—

"(5) A restraint order—

    (a) may be discharged or varied in relation to any property, and

    (b) shall be discharged on the conclusion of the proceedings or of the application in question.".

(7) In section 9 of the Act of 1986 (charging orders), the following subsection shall be substituted for subsection (7)—

"(7) In relation to a charging order, the court—

    (a) may make an order discharging or varying it, and

    (b) shall make an order discharging it—

        (i) on the conclusion of the proceedings or of the application in question, or

       (ii) on payment into court of the amount payment of which is secured by the charge.".

(8) In section 11 of the Act of 1986 (realisation of property), the following subsection shall be substituted for subsection (1)—

   "(1) Where a confiscation order—

     (a) has been made under this Act,

     (b) is not satisfied, and

     (c) is not subject to appeal,

the High Court or a county court may, on an application by the prosecutor, exercise the powers conferred by subsections (2) to (6) below.".

(9) In section 15 of the Act of 1986 (bankruptcy of defendant), the following shall be substituted for paragraphs (a) and (b) of subsection (6)—

   "(a) no order shall be made under section 339 or 423 of that Act (avoidance of certain transactions) in respect of the making of the gift at any time when—

     (i) proceedings for a drug trafficking offence have been instituted against him and have not been concluded;

    (ii) an application has been made in respect of the defendant under section 4A, 5A, 5B or 5C of this Act or section 16 of the Criminal Justice (International Co-operation) Act 1990 and has not been concluded; or

    (iii) property of the person to whom the gift was made is subject to a restraint order or charging order; and

   (b) any order made under section 339 or 423 after the conclusion of the proceedings or of the application shall take into account any realisation under this Act of property held by the person to whom the gift was made.".

(10) In section 16 of the Act of 1986 (sequestration in Scotland), the following shall be substituted for paragraphs (a) and (b) of subsection (6)—

   "(a) no decree shall be granted under section 34 or 36 of that Act (gratuitous alienations and unfair preferences) in respect of the making of the gift at any time when—

     (i) proceedings for a drug trafficking offence have been instituted against him and have not been concluded;

    (ii) an application has been made in respect of the defendant under section 4A, 5A, 5B or 5C of this Act or section 16 of the Criminal Justice (International Co-operation) Act 1990 and has not been concluded; or

    (iii) property of the person to whom the gift was made is subject to a restraint order or charging order; and

   (b) any decree made under section 34 or 36 after the conclusion of the proceedings or of the application shall take into account any realisation under this Act of property held by a person to whom the gift was made.".

(11) In section 38 of the Act of 1986 (interpretation), the following subsections shall be substituted for subsection (12)—

   "(12) Proceedings for a drug trafficking offence are concluded—

     (a) when the defendant is acquitted on all counts;

     (b) if he is convicted on one or more counts, but the court decides not to make a confiscation order against him, when it makes that decision, or

(c) if a confiscation order is made against him in those proceedings, when the order is satisfied.

(12A) An application under section 4A, 5A or 5B of this Act is concluded—

(a) if the court decides not to make a confiscation order against the defendant, when it makes that decision; or

(b) if a confiscation order is made against him as a result of that application, when the order is satisfied.

(12B) An application under section 16 of the Criminal Justice (International Co-operation) Act 1990 (increase in realisable property) or section 5C of this Act is concluded—

(a) if the court decides not to vary the confiscation order in question, when it makes that decision; or

(b) if the court varies the confiscation order as a result of the application, when the order is satisfied.

(12C) For the purposes of this Act, a confiscation order is satisfied when no amount is due under it.

(12D) For the purposes of sections 15 and 16 of this Act, a confiscation order is also satisfied when the defendant in respect of whom it was made has served a term of imprisonment or detention in default of payment of the amount due under the order.".

Death or absence of defendant

Defendant who has died or absconded

14. The following section shall be inserted in the Drug Trafficking Offences Act after section 4—

"Powers of High Court where defendant has died or absconded

4A.—(1) Subsection (2) below applies where a person has been convicted of one or more drug trafficking offences.

(2) If the prosecutor asks it to proceed under this section, the High Court may exercise the powers of the Crown Court under this Act to make a confiscation order against the defendant if satisfied that the defendant has died or absconded.

(3) Subsection (4) below applies where proceedings for one or more drug trafficking offences have been instituted against a person but have not been concluded.

(4) If the prosecutor asks it to proceed under this section, the High Court may exercise the powers of the Crown Court under this Act to make a confiscation order against the defendant if satisfied that the defendant has absconded.

(5) The power conferred by subsection (4) above may not be exercised at any time before the end of the period of two years beginning with the date which is, in the opinion of the court, the date on which the defendant absconded.

(6) In any proceedings on an application under this section—

(a) sections 2(2) and 3(1D), (2) and (3) shall not apply;

(b) the court shall not make a confiscation order against a person who has absconded unless it is satisfied that the prosecutor has taken reasonable steps to contact him, and

(c) any person appearing to the court to be likely to be affected by the making of a confiscation order by the court shall be entitled to appear before the court and make representations.".

Effect of conviction where High Court has acted under section 4A

4B.—(1) Where the High Court has made a confiscation order by virtue of section 4A of this Act, the Crown Court shall, in respect of the offence or any of the offences concerned—

(a) take account of the order before—
   (i) imposing any fine on him, or
   (ii) making any order involving any payment by him, or
   (iii) making any order under section 27 of the Misuse of Drugs Act 1971 (forfeiture orders) or section 43 of the Powers of Criminal Courts Act 1973 (deprivation orders), and

(b) subject to paragraph (a) above, leave the order out of account in determining the appropriate sentence or other manner of dealing with the defendant.

(2) Where the High Court has made a confiscation order by virtue of section 4A of this Act and the defendant subsequently appears before the Crown Court to be sentenced in respect of one or more of the offences concerned, section 1(1) of this Act shall not apply so far as his appearance is in respect of that offence or those offences.".

(2) In section 6 of the Act of 1986 (application of procedure for enforcing fines), in subsection (6), after the words "made by", where they first occur, there shall be inserted "the High Court, by virtue of section 4A of this Act, or by".

(3) The following subsection shall be added at the end of section 6 of the Act of 1986—

"(8) Where the High Court makes a confiscation order by virtue of section 4A of this Act in relation to a defendant who has died, subsection (1) above shall be read as referring only to sections 31(1) and 32(1) of the Act of 1973.".

Compensation

15. The following sections shall be inserted in the Drug Trafficking Offences Act after section 19—

"Compensation etc. where absconder is acquitted

19A.—(1) This section applies where—

(a) the High Court has made a confiscation order by virtue of section 4A(4) of this Act, and

(b) the defendant is subsequently tried for the offence or offences concerned and acquitted on all counts.

(2) The court by which the defendant is acquitted shall cancel the confiscation order.

(3) The High Court may, on the application of a person who held property which was realisable property, order compensation to be paid to the applicant if it is satisfied that the applicant has suffered loss as a result of the making of the confiscation order.

(4) The amount of compensation to be paid under this section shall be such as the court considers just in all the circumstances of the case.

(5) Rules of court may make provision—
  (a) for the giving of notice of any application under this section; and
  (b) for any person appearing to the court to be affected by any exercise of its powers under this section to be given an opportunity to make representations to the court.

(6) Any payment of compensation under this section shall be made by the Lord Chancellor out of money provided by Parliament.

(7) Where the court cancels a confiscation order under this section it may make such consequential or incidental order as it considers appropriate in connection with the cancellation.

Power to discharge confiscation order and order compensation where absconder returns

19B.—(1) This section applies where—
  (a) the High Court has made a confiscation order by virtue of section 4A(4) of this Act in relation to an absconder,
  (b) the defendant has ceased to be an absconder, and
  (c) section 19A of this Act does not apply.

(2) The High Court may, on the application of the defendant, cancel the confiscation order if it is satisfied that—
  (a) there has been undue delay in continuing the proceedings in respect of which the power under section 4A(4) of this Act was exercised; or
  (b) the prosecutor does not intend to proceed with the prosecution.

(3) Where the High Court cancels a confiscation order under this section it may, on the application of a person who held property which was realisable property, order compensation to be paid to the applicant if it is satisfied that the applicant has suffered loss as a result of the making of the confiscation order.

(4) The amount of compensation to be paid under this section shall be such as the court considers just in all the circumstances of the case.

(5) Rules of court may make provision—
  (a) for the giving of notice of any application under this section; and
  (b) for any person appearing to the court to be likely to be affected by any exercise of its powers under this section to be given an opportunity to make representations to the court.

(6) Any payment of compensation under this section shall be made by the Lord Chancellor out of money provided by Parliament.

(7) Where the court cancels a confiscation order under this section it may make such consequential or incidental order as it considers appropriate in connection with the cancellation.

Variation of confiscation orders made by virtue of section 4A

19C.—(1) This section applies where—
  (a) the High Court has made a confiscation order by virtue of section 4A(4) of this Act, and
  (b) the defendant has ceased to be an absconder.

(2) If the defendant alleges that—

(a) the value of his proceeds of drug trafficking in the period by reference to which the determination in question was made (the "original value"), or

(b) the amount that might have been realised at the time the confiscation order was made,

was less than the amount ordered to be paid under the confiscation order, he may apply to the High Court for it to consider his evidence.

(3) If, having considered that evidence, the court is satisfied that the defendant's allegation is correct it—

(a) shall make a fresh determination under subsection (4) of section 1 of this Act, and

(b) may, if it considers it just in all the circumstances, vary the amount to be recovered under the confiscation order.

(4) For any determination under section 1 of this Act by virtue of this section, section 2(5) of this Act shall not apply in relation to any of the defendant's proceeds of drug trafficking taken into account in determining the original value.

(5) Where the court varies a confiscation order under this section—

(a) it shall substitute for the term of imprisonment or of detention fixed under section 31(2) of the Powers of Criminal Courts Act 1973 in respect of the amount to be recovered under the order a shorter term determined in accordance with that section (as it has effect by virtue of section 6 of this Act) in respect of the lesser amount; and

(b) on the application of a person who held property which was realisable property, it may order compensation to be paid to the applicant if—

(i) it is satisfied that the applicant has suffered loss as a result of the making of the confiscation order; and

(ii) having regard to all the circumstances of the case, the court considers it to be appropriate.

(6) The amount of compensation to be paid under this section shall be such as the court considers just in all the circumstances of the case.

(7) Rules of court may make provision—

(a) for the giving of notice of any application under this section; and

(b) for any person appearing to the court to be likely to be affected by any exercise of its powers under this section to be given an opportunity to make representations to the court.

(8) Any payment of compensation under this section shall be made by the Lord Chancellor out of money provided by Parliament.

(9) No application shall be entertained by the court under this section if it is made after the end of the period of six years beginning with the date on which the confiscation order was made.".

Offences

Acquisition, possession or use of proceeds of drug trafficking

16.—(1) The following section shall be inserted in the Drug Trafficking Offences Act 1986 at the appropriate place—

Appendix XXXVII

"Acquiring etc. property derived from drug trafficking

Acquisition, possession or use of proceeds of drug trafficking

23A.—(1) A person is guilty of an offence if, knowing that any property is, or in whole or in part directly or indirectly represents, another person's proceeds of drug trafficking, he acquires or uses that property or has possession of it.

(2) It is a defence to a charge of committing an offence under this section that the person charged acquired or used the property or had possession of it for adequate consideration.

(3) For the purposes of subsection (2) above—
   (a) a person acquires property for adequate consideration if the value of the consideration is significantly less than the value of the property; and
   (b) a person uses or has possession of property for inadequate consideration if the value of the consideration is significantly less than the value of his use or possession of the property.

(4) The provision for any person of services or goods which are of assistance to him in drug trafficking shall not be treated as consideration for the purposes of subsection (2) above.

(5) Where a person discloses to a constable a suspicion or belief that any property is, or in whole or in part directly or indirectly represents, another person's proceeds of drug trafficking, or discloses to a constable any matter on which such a suspicion or belief is based—
   (a) the disclosure shall not be treated as a breach of any restriction upon the disclosure of information imposed by statute or otherwise; and
   (b) if he does any act in relation to the property in contravention of subsection (1) above, he does not commit an offence under this section if—
      (i) the disclosure is made before he does the act concerned and the act is done with the consent of the constable, or
      (ii) the disclosure is made after he does the act, but on his initiative and as soon as it is reasonable for him to make it.

(6) For the purposes of this section, having possession of any property shall be taken to be doing an act in relation to it.

(7) In proceedings against a person for an offence under this section, it is a defence to prove that—
   (a) he intended to disclose to a constable such suspicion, belief or matter as is mentioned in subsection (5) above, but
   (b) there is reasonable excuse for his failure to make the disclosure in accordance with paragraph (b) of that subsection.

(8) In the case of a person who was in employment at the relevant time, subsections (5) and (7) above shall have effect in relation to disclosures, and intended disclosures, to the appropriate person in accordance with the procedure established by his employer for the making of such disclosures as they have effect in relation to disclosures, and intended disclosures, to a constable.

(9) A person guilty of an offence under this section is liable—
   (a) on summary conviction, to imprisonment for a term not exceeding

six months or a fine not exceeding the statutory maximum or to both, or

(b) on conviction on indictment, to imprisonment for a term not exceeding fourteen years or a fine or to both.

(10) No constable or other person shall be guilty of an offence under this section in respect of anything done by him in the course of acting in connection with the enforcement, or intended enforcement, of any provision of this Act or of any other enactment relating to drug trafficking or the proceeds of such trafficking.".

(2) In section 2(4) of the Act of 1986 (circumstances where assumptions are not to be made), after first "section" there shall be inserted "23A or".

Acquisition, possession or use of proceeds of drug trafficking: Scotland

17.—(1) The following section shall be inserted in the Criminal Justice (Scotland) Act 1987 after section 42—

"Acquisition, possession or use of proceeds of drug trafficking

42A.—(1) A person is guilty of an offence if, knowing that any property is, or in whole or in part directly or indirectly represents, another person's proceeds of drug trafficking, he acquires or uses that property or has possession of it.

(2) It is a defence to a charge of committing an offence under this section that the person charged acquired or used the property or had possession of it for adequate consideration.

(3) For the purposes of subsection (2) above—
    (a) a person acquires property for inadequate consideration if the value of the consideration is significantly less than the value of the property; and
    (b) a person uses or has possession of property for inadequate consideration if the value of the consideration is significantly less than the value of his use or possession of the property.

(4) The provision for any person of services or goods which are of assistance to him in drug trafficking shall not be treated as consideration for the purposes of subsection (2) above.

(5) Where a person discloses to a constable or to a person commissioned by the Commissioners of Customs and Excise a suspicion or belief that any property is, or in whole or in part directly or indirectly represents, another person's proceeds of drug trafficking, or discloses to a constable or a person so commissioned any matter on which such a suspicion or belief is based—
    (a) the disclosure shall not be treated as a breach of any restriction upon the disclosure of information imposed by statute or otherwise; and
    (b) if he does any act in relation to the property in contravention of subsection (1) above, he does not commit an offence under this section if—
        (i) the disclosure is made before he does the act concerned and the act is done with the consent of the constable or person so commissioned, or
        (ii) the disclosure is made after he does the act, but on his initiative and as soon as it is reasonable for him to make it.

(6) For the purposes of this section having possession of any property shall be taken to be doing an act in relation to it.

(7) In proceedings against a person for an offence under this section, it is a defence to prove that—

(a) he intended to disclose to a constable or a person so commissioned such a suspicion, belief or matter as is mentioned in subsection (5) above; but

(b) there is reasonable excuse for his failure to make the disclosure in accordance with paragraph (b) of that subsection.

(8) In the case of a person who was in employment at the relevant time, subsections (5) and (7) above shall have effect in relation to disclosures, and intended disclosures, to the appropriate person in accordance with the procedure established by his employer for the making of such disclosures as they have effect in relation to disclosures, and intended disclosures, to a constable or a person so commissioned.

(9) A person guilty of an offence under this section is liable—

(a) on summary conviction, to imprisonment for a term not exceeding six months or to a fine not exceeding the statutory maximum or to both; or

(b) on conviction on indictment, to imprisonment for a term not exceeding fourteen years or to a fine or to both.

(10) No constable, person so commissioned or other person shall be guilty of an offence under this section in respect of anything done by him in the course of acting in connection with the enforcement, or intended enforcement, of any provision of this Act or of any other enactment relating to drug trafficking or the proceeds of such trafficking.

(2) In section 3(3) of the Act of 1987 (circumstances where assumptions are not to be made), after the word "section" where it first occurs there shall be inserted the words "42A or".

Offences in connection with laundering money from drug trafficking

18.—(1) The following sections shall be inserted in the Drug Trafficking Offences Act 1986, after section 26A—

"Offences in connection with money laundering

Failure to disclose knowledge or suspicion of money laundering

26B.—(1) A person is guilty of an offence if—

(a) he knows, or suspects, that another person is engaged in drug money laundering,

(b) the information, or other matter, on which that knowledge or suspicion is based came to his attention in the course of his trade, profession, business or employment, and

(c) he does not disclose the information or other matter to a constable as soon as is reasonably practicable after it comes to his attention.

(2) Subsection (1) above does not make it an offence for a professional legal adviser to fail to disclose any information or other matter which has come to him in privileged circumstances.

(3) It is a defence to a charge of committing an offence under this section that the person charged had a reasonable excuse for not disclosing the information or other matter in question.

(4) Where a person discloses to a constable—
- (a) his suspicion or belief that another person is engaged in drug money laundering, or
- (b) any information or other matter on which that suspicion or belief is based,

the disclosure shall not be treated as a breach of any restriction imposed by statute or otherwise.

(5) Without prejudice to subsection (3) or (4) above, in the case of a person who was in employment at the relevant time, it is a defence to a charge of committing an offence under this section that he disclosed the information or other matter in question to the appropriate person in accordance with the procedure established by his employer for the making of such disclosures.

(6) A disclosure to which subsection (5) applies shall not be treated as a breach of any restriction imposed by statute or otherwise.

(7) In this section, "drug money laundering" means doing any act which constitutes an offence under—
- (a) section 23A or 24 of this Act; or
- (b) section 14 of the Criminal Justice (International Co-operation) Act 1990 (concealing or transferring proceeds of drug trafficking;

or, in the case of an act done otherwise than in England and Wales, would constitute such an offence if done in England and Wales.

(8) For the purposes of subsection (7) above, having possession of any property shall be taken to be doing an act in relation to it.

(9) For the purposes of this section, any information or other matter comes to a professional legal adviser in privileged circumstances if it is communicated, or given, to him—
- (a) by, or by a representative of, a client of his in connection with the giving by the adviser of legal advice to the client;
- (b) by, or by a representative of, a person seeking legal advice from the adviser; or
- (c) by any person—
  - (i) in contemplation of, or in connection with, legal proceedings; and
  - (ii) for the purpose of those proceedings.

(10) No information or other matter shall be treated as coming to a professional legal adviser in privileged circumstances if it is communicated or given with a view to furthering any criminal purpose.

(11) A person guilty of an offence under this section shall be liable—
- (a) on summary conviction, to imprisonment for a term not exceeding six months or a fine not exceeding the statutory maximum or to both, or
- (b) on conviction on indictment, to imprisonment for a term not exceeding five years or a fine, or to both.

Tipping-off

26C.—(1) A person is guilty of an offence if—
- (a) he knows or suspects that a constable is acting, or is proposing to act, in connection with an investigation which is being, or is about to be, conducted into drug money laundering, and
- (b) he discloses to any other person information or any other matter

which is likely to prejudice that investigation, or proposed investigation.

(2) A person is guilty of an offence if—

(a) he knows or suspects that a disclosure ("the disclosure") has been made to a constable under section 23A, 24 or 26B of this Act, and

(b) he discloses to any other person information or any other matter which is likely to prejudice any investigation which might be conducted following the disclosure.

(3) A person is guilty of an offence if—

(a) he knows or suspects that a disclosure of a kind mentioned in section 23A(8), 24(4A) or 26B(5) of this Act ("the disclosure") has been made, and

(b) he discloses to any person information or any other matter which is likely to prejudice any investigation which might be conducted following the disclosure.

(4) Nothing in subsections (1) to (3) above makes it an offence for a professional legal adviser to disclose any information or other matter—

(a) to, or to a representative, of a client of his in connection with the giving by the adviser of legal advice to the client; or

(b) to any person—

   (i) in contemplation of, or in connection with, legal proceedings; and

   (ii) for the purpose of those proceedings.

(5) Subsection (4) above does not apply in relation to any information or other matter which is disclosed with a view to furthering any criminal purpose.

(6) In proceedings against a person for an offence under subsection (1), (2) or (3) above, it is a defence to prove that he did not know or suspect that the disclosure was likely to be prejudicial in the way mentioned in that subsection.

(7) In this section "drug money laundering" and "item subject to legal privilege" have the same meaning as in section 26B above.

(8) A person guilty of an offence under this section shall be liable—

(a) on summary conviction, to imprisonment for a term not exceeding six months or a fine not exceeding the statutory maximum or to both, or

(b) on conviction on indictment, to imprisonment for a term not exceeding five years or a fine or to both.

(9) No constable or other person shall be guilty of an offence under this section in respect of anything done by him in the course of acting in connection with the enforcement, or intended enforcement, of any provision of this Act or of any other enactment relating to drug trafficking or the proceeds of such trafficking."

(2) In section 24 of the Drug Trafficking Offences Act 1986 (assisting another to retain the benefit of drug trafficking), in subsection (3)(a), for the word "contract" there shall be substituted "statute or otherwise".

(3) In section 24 of the Act of 1986, the following subsection shall be inserted after subsection (4)—

"(4A) In the case of a person who was in employment at the relevant time, subsections (3) and (4) above shall have effect in relation to disclosures, and intended disclosures, to the appropriate person in accordance with the procedure established by his employer for the making of such disclosures as they have effect in relation to disclosures, and intended disclosures, to a constable.".

Offences in connection with laundering money from drug trafficking: Scotland

19.—(1) The following sections shall be inserted after section 43 of the Criminal Justice (Scotland) Act 1987—

"Failure to disclose knowledge or suspicion of money laundering

43A.—(1) A person is guilty of an offence if—
  (a) he knows, or suspects, that another person is engaged in drug money laundering,
  (b) the information, or other matter, on which that knowledge or suspicion is based came to his attention in the course of his trade, profession, business or employment, and
  (c) he does not disclose the information or other matter to a constable or to a person commissioned by the Commissioners of Customs and Excise as soon as is reasonably practicable after it comes to his attention.

(2) Subsection (1) above does not make it an offence for a professional legal adviser to fail to disclose any information or other matter which has come to him in privileged circumstances.

(3) It is a defence to a charge of committing an offence under this section that the person charged had a reasonable excuse for not disclosing the information or other matter in question.

(4) Where a person discloses to a constable or a person so commissioned—
  (a) his suspicion or belief that another person is engaged in drug money laundering, or
  (b) any information or other matter on which that suspicion or belief is based,
the disclosure shall not be treated as a breach of any restriction imposed by statute or otherwise.

(5) Without prejudice to subsection (3) or (4) above, in the case of a person who was in employment at the relevant time, it is a defence to a charge of committing an offence under this section that he disclosed the information or other matter in question to the appropriate person in accordance with the procedure established by his employer for the making of such disclosures.

(6) A disclosure to which subsection (5) above applies shall not be treated as a breach of any restriction imposed by statute or otherwise.

(7) In this section "drug money laundering" means doing any act which constitutes an offence under—
  (a) section 42A or 43 of this Act; or
  (b) section 14 of the Criminal Justice (International Co-operation) Act 1990 (concealing or transferring proceeds of drug trafficking),
or, in the case of an act done otherwise than in Scotland, would constitute such an offence if done in Scotland.

(8) For the purposes of subsection (7) above, having possession of any property shall be taken to be doing an act in relation to it.

(9) For the purposes of this section, any information or other matter

comes to a professional legal adviser in privileged circumstances if it is communicated, or given, to him—

(a) by, or by a representative of, a client of his in connection with the giving by the adviser of legal advice to the client;

(b) by, or by a representative of, a person seeking legal advice from the adviser; or

(c) by any person—

    (i) in contemplation of, or in connection with, legal proceedings; and

    (ii) for the purpose of those proceedings.

(10) No information or other matter shall be treated as coming to a professional legal adviser in privileged circumstances if it is communicated or given with a view to furthering any criminal purpose.

(11) A person guilty of an offence under this section shall be liable—

(a) on summary conviction, to imprisonment for a term not exceeding six months or a fine not exceeding the statutory maximum or to both, or

(b) on conviction on indictment, to imprisonment for a term not exceeding five years or a fine, or to both.

Tipping-off

43B.—(1) A person is guilty of an offence if—

(a) he knows or suspects that a constable or a person commissioned by the Commissioners of Customs and Excise is acting, or is proposing to act, in connection with an investigation which is being, or is about to be, conducted into drug money laundering within the meaning of subsections (7) (8) of section 43A of this Act, and

(b) he discloses to any other person information or any other matter which is likely to prejudice that investigation, or proposed investigation.

(2) A person is guilty of an offence if—

(a) he knows or suspects that a disclosure has been made to a constable, or a person so commissioned, under section 42A, 43 or 43A of this Act; and

(b) he discloses to any other person information or any other matter which is likely to prejudice any investigation which might be conducted following the disclosure.

(3) A person is guilty of an offence if—

(a) he knows or suspects that a disclosure of a kind mentioned in section 42A(8), 43(4A) or 43A(5) of this Act has been made; and

(b) he discloses to any person information or any other matter which is likely to prejudice any investigation which might be conducted following the disclosure.

(4) Nothing in subsections (1) to (3) above makes it an offence for a professional legal adviser to disclose any information or other matter—

(a) to, or to a representative of, a client of his in connection with the giving by the adviser of legal advice to the client; or

(b) to any person—

    (i) in contemplation of, or in connection with, legal proceedings; and

    (ii) for the purpose of those proceedings.

(5) Subsection (4) above does not apply in relation to any information or other matter which is disclosed with a view to furthering any criminal purpose.

(6) In proceedings against a person for an offence under subsection (1), (2) or (3) above, it is a defence to prove that he did not know or suspect that the disclosure was likely to be prejudicial in the way mentioned in that subsection.

(7) A person guilty of an offence under this section shall be liable—

    (a) on summary conviction, to imprisonment for a term not exceeding six months or a fine not exceeding the statutory maximum or to both, or

    (b) on conviction on indictment, to imprisonment for a term not exceeding five years or a fine, or to both.

(8) No constable, person so commissioned or other person shall be guilty of an offence under this section in respect of anything done by him in the course of acting in connection with the enforcement, or intended enforcement, of any provision of this Act or of any other enactment relating to drug trafficking or the proceeds of such trafficking.".

(2) In section 43 of the Act of 1987 (assisting another to retain the proceeds of drug trafficking)—

    (a) in subsection (3), after the words "trafficking or" there shall be inserted the words "discloses to a constable or a person so commissioned"; and

    (b) in paragraph (a) of subsection (3), for the word "contract" there shall be substituted the words "statute or otherwise,".

(3) After subsection (4) of that section, there shall be inserted the following subsection—

"(4A) In the case of a person who was in employment at the relevant time, subsections (3) and (4) above shall have effect in relation to disclosures, and intended disclosures, to the appropriate person in accordance with the procedure established by his employer for the making of such disclosures as they have effect in relation to disclosures, and intended disclosures, to a constable or a person commissioned as aforesaid.".

Prosecution by order of the Commissioners of Customs and Excise

20.—(1) The following section shall be inserted in the Drug Trafficking Offences Act 1986, after section 36—

"Prosecution by order of the Commissioners of Customs and Excise

36A.—(1) Proceedings for an offence to which this section applies ("a specified offence") may be instituted by order of the Commissioners.

(2) Any proceedings for a specified offence which are so instituted shall be commenced in the name of an officer.

(3) In the case of the death, removal, discharge or absence of the officer in whose name any proceedings for a specified offence were commenced, those proceedings may be continued by another officer.

(4) Where the Commissioners investigate, or propose to investigate, any matter with a view to determining—

    (a) whether there are grounds for believing that a specified offence has been committed, or

    (b) whether a person should be prosecuted for a specified offence, that matter shall be treated as an assigned matter within the meaning of the Customs and Excise Management Act 1979.

(5) Nothing in this section shall be taken—

(a) to prevent any person (including any officer) who has power to arrest, detain or prosecute any person for a specified offence from doing so; or

(b) to prevent a court from proceeding to deal with a person brought before it following his arrest by an officer for a specified offence, even though the proceedings have not been instituted by an order made under subsection (1) above.

(6) In this section—

"the Commissioners" means the Commissioners of Customs and Excise;

"officer" means a person commissioned by the Commissioners; and "specified offence" means—

(a) an offence under section 23A, 24, 26B, 26C or 31 of this Act or section 14 of the Criminal Justice (International Co-operation) Act 1990 (concealing or transferring proceeds of drug trafficking);

(b) attempting to commit, conspiracy to commit or incitement to commit any such offence; or

(c) any other offence of a kind prescribed in regulations made by the Secretary of State for the purposes of this section.

(7) The power to make regulations under subsection (6) above shall be exercisable by statutory instrument.

(8) Any such instrument shall be subject to annulment in pursuance of a resolution of either House of Parliament.".

(2) The following section shall be inserted in the Criminal Justice (Scotland) Act 1987 after section 40—

"Prosecution by order of the Commissioners and Customs and Excise

40A.—(1) Summary proceedings for a specified offence may be instituted by order of the Commissioners and shall, if so instituted, be commenced in the name of an officer.

(2) In the case of the death, removal, discharge or absence of the officer in whose name any proceedings for a specified offence were commenced, those proceedings may be continued by another officer.

(3) Where the Commissioners investigate, or propose to investigate, any matter with a view to determining—

(a) whether there are grounds for believing that a specified offence has been committed, or

(b) whether a person should be prosecuted for a specified offence,

that matter shall be treated as an assigned matter within the meaning of the Customs and Excise Management Act 1979.

(4) Nothing in this section shall be taken—

(a) to prevent any person (including any officer) who has power to arrest, detain or prosecute any person for a specified offence from doing so; or

(b) to prevent a court from proceeding to deal with a person brought before it following his arrest by an officer for a specified offence, even though the proceedings have not been instituted by an order made under subsection (1) above.

(5) In this section—

"the Commissioners" means the Commissioners of Customs and Excise;

"officer" means an officer commissioned by the Commissioners; and

"specified offence" means—

  (a) an offence under section 42, 42A, 43, 43A or 43B of this Act or section 14 of the Criminal Justice (International Co-operation) Act 1990 (concealing or transferring proceeds of drug trafficking);

  (b) attempting to commit, conspiracy to commit or incitement to commit any such offence; or

  (c) any other offence of a kind prescribed in regulations made by the Secretary of State for the purposes of this section.

(6) Regulations under subsection (5) above shall be made by statutory instrument subject to annulment in pursuance of a resolution of either House of Parliament.".

Enforcement

Enforcement of certain orders

21.—(1) In section 9 of the Criminal Justice (International Co-operation) Act 1990 (enforcement of overseas forfeiture orders), in subsection (1)(b), the words "or intended for use" shall be inserted after "used",

(2) In section 24A of the Drug Trafficking Offences Act 1986 (recognition and enforcement of certain orders), the following shall be substituted for subsection (6)—

  "(6) An Order in Council under this section shall be subject to annulment in pursuance of a resolution of either House of Parliament.".

(3) The same subsection as is inserted in section 24A of the Act of 1986 by subsection (2) shall be inserted in—

  (a) section 25 of that Act (but in substitution for subsection (4));

  (b) section 26 of that Act (but in substitution for subsection (5));

  (c) section 29 of the Criminal Justice (Scotland) Act 1987 (but in substitution for subsection (4));

  (d) section 30 of the Act of 1987 (but in substitution for subsection (5));

  (e) section 94 of the Criminal Justice Act 1988 (but in substitution for subsection (4));

  (f) section 95 of the Act of 1988 (but in substitution for subsection (3));

  (g) section 96 of the Act of 1988 (but in substitution for subsection (5));

  (h) section 9 of the Criminal Justice (International Co-operation) Act 1990 (but in substitution for subsection (5)).

Enforcement of Northern Ireland orders: drug trafficking

22.—(1) In section 25 of the Drug Trafficking Offences Act 1986 (enforcement of Northern Ireland orders), in subsection (1), for "19" there shall be substituted "18" and the following subsection shall be inserted after subsection (3)—

  "(3A) An Order in Council under this section may, in particular, provide for section 18 of the Civil Jurisdiction and Judgments Act 1982 (enforcement of United Kingdom judgments in other parts of the United Kingdom) not to apply in relation to such orders as may be prescribed by the Order.".

(2) In section 29 of the Criminal Justice (Scotland) Act 1987 (enforcement of Northern Ireland orders), the following subsection shall be inserted after subsection (3)—

"(3A) An Order in Council under this section may, in particular, provide for section 18 of the Civil Jurisdiction and Judgments Act 1982 (enforcement of United Kingdom judgments in other parts of the United Kingdom) not to apply in relation to such orders as may be prescribed by the Order.".

Transfer of certain enforcement powers to Commissioners of Customs and Excise

23.—(1) The functions of the Secretary of State under section 20 of the Criminal Justice (International Co-operation) Act 1990 (enforcement powers in relation to ships) are transferred to the Commissioners of Customs and Excise.

(2) The following consequential amendments shall be made in the Act of 1990—

  (a) in section 20, for "Secretary of State", "he" and "his", wherever they occur, there shall be substituted, respectively, "Commissioners of Customs and Excise", "they" and "their";

  (b) in section 21(3), for "Secretary of State", where first occurring, there shall be substituted "Commissioners of Customs and Excise"; and

  (c) in paragraph 2(2) of Schedule 3, for "Secretary of State" there shall be substituted "Commissioners of Customs and Excise".

(3) The transfer of functions effected by this section shall not affect the validity of any action taken or begun under section 20 of the Act of 1990 before the coming into force of this section.

Miscellaneous

Miscellaneous amendments

24.—(1) In section 8(6) of the Drug Trafficking Offences Act 1986 (restraint orders), for "the court may" there shall be substituted "the High Court or a county court may".

(2) In sections 12(1) and (2), 13(1), 15(2), 16(2), 17(2) and 19(2)(b)(i) of that Act after "High Court" there shall be inserted, in each case, "or a county court".

(3) In section 17A(2) of that Act (expenses of insolvency practitioner dealing with property subject to restraint order), for "(3)(za)" there shall be substituted "(4)".

(4) In section 18(2) of that Act (remuneration and expenses of receiver), for "(3B)" there shall be substituted "(5)".

(5) In section 27 of that Act (application for an order to make material available), in subsection (8) for "this section" there shall be substituted "subsection (1) above" and the following subsection shall be added at the end—

  "(10) An application under subsection (1) or (5) above may be made ex parte to a judge in chambers."

(6) In section 27(5) of that Act the words "or, as the case may be, the sheriff" (which are spent) shall be omitted.

(7) Section 38(1) of that Act (interpretation) shall be amended in accordance with subsections (8) and (9).

(8) In the definition of "drug trafficking", in paragraph (d) the words "or would

be such an offence if it took place in England and Wales" shall be inserted at the end and the following paragraphs shall be inserted after paragraph (d)—

"(e) acquiring, having possession or using property in circumstances which amount to the commission of an offence under section 23A of this Act or which would be such an offence if it took place in England and Wales;

(f) conduct which is an offence under section 14 (concealing or transferring proceeds of drug trafficking) of the Criminal Justice (International Co-operation) Act 1990 or which would be such an offence if it took place in England and Wales;

(g) using any ship for illicit traffic in controlled drugs in circumstances which amount to the commission of an offence under section 19 of the Act of 1990;".

(9) In the definition of "drug trafficking offence", the following paragraph shall be inserted after paragraph (c)—

"(cc) an offence under section 23A of this Act;".

(10) In section 18(4A) of the Civil Jurisdiction and Judgments Act 1982 (enforcement of United Kingdom judgments in other parts of the United Kingdom), after "High Court" there shall be inserted "or a county court".

(11) In section 116(2)(aa) of the Police and Criminal Evidence Act 1984 (drug trafficking offences to be arrestable offences that are always serious), for "(d)" there shall be substituted "(dd)".

(12) Section 1 of the Criminal Justice (Scotland) Act 1987 (confiscation orders in relation to drug trafficking offences) shall be amended in accordance with subsections (13) to (15).

(13) In subsection (2) (offences in relation to which confiscation orders may be made), the following paragraph shall be inserted after paragraph (b)—

"(bb) an offence under section 42A of this Act;".

(14) In subsection (6) (definition of "drug trafficking"), after paragraph (e) there shall be inserted the following paragraphs—

"(f) acquiring, having possession of or using property in contravention of section 42A of this Act;

(g) concealing or transferring the proceeds of drug trafficking in contravention of section 14 of the Act of 1990;

(h) using any ship for illicit traffic in controlled drugs in contravention of section 19 of the Act of 1990;".

(15) After subsection (6) there shall be inserted the following subsection—

"(7) In paragraphs (e) to (g) of subsection (6) above, references to conduct in contravention of the enactments mentioned in those paragraphs include conduct which would contravene the enactments if it took place in Scotland.".

Appeal against order forfeiting drug trafficking cash

25.—(1) The following sections shall be inserted in the Criminal Justice (International Co-operation) Act 1990, after section 26—

"Appeal against section 26 order

26A.—(1) This section applies where an order for the forfeiture of cash ("the forfeiture order") is made under section 26 above by a magistrates' court.

(2) Any party to the proceedings in which the forfeiture order is made (other than the applicant for the order) may, before the end of the period of 30 days beginning with the date on which it is made, appeal to the Crown Court or, in Northern Ireland, to a county court.

(3) An appeal under this section shall be by way of a rehearing.

(4) On an application made by the appellant to a magistrates' court at any time, that court may order the release of so much of the cash to which the forfeiture order relates as it considers appropriate to enable him to meet his legal expenses in connection with the appeal.

(5) The court hearing an appeal under this section may make such order as it considers appropriate.

(6) If it upholds the appeal, the court may order the release of the cash, or (as the case may be) the remaining cash, together with any accrued interest.

(7) Section 26(3) applies in relation to a rehearing on an appeal under this section as it applies to proceedings under section 26.

Appeal against section 26 order: Scotland

26B. Any party to proceedings in which an order for the forfeiture of cash is made by the sheriff under section 26 above may appeal against the order to the Court of Session.".

(2) The Act of 1990 shall be further amended as follows.

(3) In section 26 (forfeiture of drug trafficking cash), after subsection (3) there shall be inserted the following subsection—

"(4) Proceedings on an application under this section to the sheriff shall be civil proceedings.".

(4) In section 28 (procedure), the words "appeals" shall be inserted after the word "applications" in each place where it occurs in subsection (2).

(5) In section 30 (forfeited cash to be paid into the Consolidated Fund), the following subsection shall be added at the end—

"(3) Subsection (2) above does not apply—
   (a) where an appeal is made under section 26A or 26B above, before the appeal is determined or otherwise disposed of; and
   (b) in any other case—
      (i) where the forfeiture was ordered by a magistrates' court, before the end of the period of 30 days mentioned in section 26A(2); or
      (ii) where the forfeiture was ordered by the sheriff, before the end of any period within which, in accordance with rules of court, an appeal under section 26B must be made.".

(6) The amendments made by this section apply only in relation to orders under section 26 of the Act of 1990 made on or after the date on which this section comes into force.

Disclosure of information etc. received in privileged circumstances

26.—(1) In section 31 of the Drug Trafficking Offences Act 1986 (offence of prejudicing investigation), the following subsections shall be inserted after subsection (2)—

"(2A) Nothing in subsection (1) above makes it an offence for a professional legal adviser to disclose any information or other matter—

(a) to, or to a representative of, a client of his in connection with the giving by the adviser of legal advice to the client; or

(b) to any person—

(i) in contemplation of, or in connection with, legal proceedings; and

(ii) for the purpose of those proceedings.

(2B) Subsection (2A) above does not apply in relation to any information or other matter which is disclosed with a view to furthering any criminal purpose.".

(2) The same subsections as are inserted in section 31 of the Act of 1986 by subsection (1) shall be inserted in section 42 of the Criminal Justice (Scotland) Act 1987 (corresponding Scottish provision).

PART III

PROCEEDS OF CRIMINAL CONDUCT

Confiscation orders

Confiscation orders

27.—(1) Section 71 of the Criminal Justice Act 1988 (confiscation orders) shall be amended as follows.

(2) The following subsection shall be inserted after subsection (7)—

"(7A) The standard of proof required to determine any question arising under this Part of this Act as to—

(a) whether a person has benefited as mentioned in subsection (2)(b)(i) above;

(b) whether his benefit is at least the minimum amount; or

(c) the amount to be recovered in his case by virtue of section 72 below, shall be that applicable in civil proceedings.".

(3) The following subsection shall be inserted at the end—

"(10) Subsection (9) above is subject to section 93E below.".

Postponed determinations

28. The following section shall be inserted in the Criminal Justice Act 1988, after section 72—

Postponed determinations

72A.—(1) Where a court is acting under section 71 above but considers that it requires further information before—

(a) determining whether the defendant has benefited as mentioned in section 71(2)(b)(i) above;

(b) determining whether his benefit is at least the minimum amount; or

(c) determining the amount to be recovered in his case by virtue of section 72 above,

it may, for the purpose of enabling that information to be obtained, postpone making that determination for such period as it may specify.

(2) More than one postponement may be made under subsection (1) above in relation to the same case.

(3) Unless it is satisfied that there are exceptional circumstances, the court shall not specify a period under subsection (1) above which—

(a) by itself; or

(b) where there have been one or more previous postponements under subsection (1) above or (4) below, when taken together with the earlier specified period or periods,

exceeds six months beginning with the date of conviction.

(4) Where the defendant appeals against his conviction, the court may, on that account—

(a) postpone making any of the determinations mentioned in subsection (1) above for such period as it may specify; or

(b) where it has already exercised its powers under this section to postpone, extend the specified period.

(5) A postponement or extension under subsection (1) or (4) above may be made—

(a) on application by the defendant or the prosecutor; or

(b) by the court of its own motion.

(6) Unless the court is satisfied that there are exceptional circumstances, any postponement or extension under subsection (4) above shall not exceed the period ending three months after the date on which the appeal is determined or otherwise disposed of.

(7) Where the court exercises its power under subsection (1) or (4) above, it may nevertheless proceed to sentence, or otherwise deal with, the defendant in respect of the offence or any of the offences concerned.

(8) Where the court has so proceeded, section 72 above shall have effect as if—

(a) in subsection (4), the words from "before sentencing" to "offences concerned" were omitted; and

(b) in subsection (5), after "determining" there were inserted "in relation to any offence in respect of which he has not been sentenced or otherwise dealt with".

(9) In sentencing, or otherwise dealing with, the defendant in respect of the offence, or any of the offences, concerned at any time during the specified period, the court shall not—

(a) impose any fine on him; or

(b) make any such order as is mentioned in section 72(5)(b) or (c) above.

(10) In this section, references to an appeal include references to an application under section 111 of the Magistrates' Courts Act 1980 (statement of case by magistrates' court).

(11) In this section "the date of conviction" means—

(a) the date on which the defendant was convicted of the offence concerned, or

(b) where he was convicted in the same proceedings, but on different dates, of two or more offences which may be taken together for the purposes of subsection (2) or, as the case may be, (3) of section 71 above, the date of the latest of those convictions.".

Money laundering and other offences

Assisting another to retain the benefit of criminal conduct

29.—(1) The following section shall be inserted in the Criminal Justice Act 1988, after section 93—

"Money laundering and other offences

Assisting another to retain the benefit of criminal conduct

93A.—(1) Subject to subsection (3) below, if a person enters into or is otherwise concerned in an arrangement whereby—

(a) the retention or control by or on behalf of another ("A") of A's proceeds of criminal conduct is facilitated (whether by concealment, removal from the jurisdiction, transfer to nominees or otherwise); or

(b) A's proceeds of criminal conduct—

    (i) are used to secure that funds are placed at A's disposal; or

    (ii) are used for A's benefit to acquire property by way of investment,

knowing or suspecting that A is a person who is or has been engaged in criminal conduct or has benefited from criminal conduct, he is guilty of an offence.

(2) In this section, references to any person's proceeds of criminal conduct include a reference to any property which in whole or in part directly or indirectly represented in his hands his proceeds of criminal conduct.

(3) Where a person discloses to a constable a suspicion or belief that any funds or investments are derived from or used in connection with criminal conduct or discloses to a constable any matter on which such a suspicion or belief is based—

(a) the disclosure shall not be treated as a breach of any restriction upon the disclosure of information imposed by statute or otherwise; and

(b) if he does any act in contravention of subsection (1) above and the disclosure relates to the arrangement concerned, he does not commit an offence under this section if—

    (i) the disclosure is made before he does the act concerned and the act is done with the consent of the constable; or

    (ii) the disclosure is made after he does the act, but is made on his initiative and as soon as it is reasonable for him to make it.

(4) In proceedings against a person for an offence under this section, it is a defence to prove—

(a) that he did not know or suspect that the arrangement related to any person's proceeds of criminal conduct; or

(b) that he did not know or suspect that by the arrangement the retention or control by or on behalf of A of any property was facilitated or, as the case may be, that by the arrangement any property was used, as mentioned in subsection (a) above; or

(c) that—

    (i) he intended to disclose to a constable such a suspicion, belief or matter as is mentioned in subsection (3) above in relation to the arrangement; but

    (ii) there is reasonable excuse for his failure to make disclosure in accordance with subsection (3)(b) above.

(5) In the case of a person who was in employment at the relevant time, subsections (3) and (4) above shall have effect in relation to disclosures, and intended disclosures, to the appropriate person in accordance with the procedure established by his employer for the making of such disclosures as

they have effect in relation to disclosures, and intended disclosures, to a constable.

(6) A person guilty of an offence under this section shall be liable—

(a) on summary conviction, to imprisonment for a term not exceeding six months or a fine not exceeding the statutory maximum or to both; or

(b) on conviction on indictment, to imprisonment for a term not exceeding fourteen years or a fine or to both.

(7) In this Part of this Act "criminal conduct" means conduct which constitutes an offence to which this Part of this Act applies or would constitute such an offence if it had occurred in England and Wales or (as the case may be) Scotland.".

(2) In section 102(1) of the Act of 1988 (interpretation of Part VI), the following definition shall be inserted after the definition of "interest"—

" "proceeds of criminal conduct", in relation to any person who has benefited from criminal conduct, means that benefit;".

(3) In section 102(2) of the Act of 1988, the following entry shall be inserted in the table after the entry relating to section 71(9)(a)—

"Criminal conduct   Section 93A(7)".

Acquisition, possession or use of proceeds of criminal conduct

30. The following section shall be inserted in the Criminal Justice Act 1988, after section 93A—

"Acquisition, possession or use of proceeds of criminal conduct

93B.—(1) A person is guilty of an offence if, knowing that any property is, or in whole or in part directly or indirectly represents, another person's proceeds of criminal conduct, he acquires or uses that property or has possession of it.

(2) It is a defence to a charge of committing an offence under this section that the person charged acquired or used the property or had possession of it for adequate consideration.

(3) For the purposes of subsection (2) above—

(a) a person acquires property for inadequate consideration if the value of the consideration is significantly less than the value of the property; and

(b) a person uses or has possession of property for inadequate consideration if the value of the consideration is significantly less than the value of his use or possession of the property.

(4) The provision for any person of services or goods which are of assistance to him in criminal conduct shall not be treated as consideration for the purposes of subsection (2) above.

(5) Where a person discloses to a constable a suspicion or belief that any property is, or in whole or in part directly or indirectly represents, another person's proceeds of criminal conduct or discloses to a constable any matter on which such a suspicion or belief is based—

(a) the disclosure shall not be treated as a breach of any restriction upon the disclosure of information imposed by statute or otherwise; and

(b) if he does any act in relation to that property in contravention of subsection (1) above, he does not commit an offence under this section if—

    (i) the disclosure is made before he does the act concerned and the act is done with the consent of the constable; or

    (ii) the disclosure is made after he does the act, but on his initiative and as soon as it is reasonable for him to make it.

(6) For the purposes of this section, having possession of any property shall be taken to be doing an act in relation to it.

(7) In proceedings against a person for an offence under this section, it is a defence to prove that—

    (a) he intended to disclose to a constable such a suspicion, belief or matter as is mentioned in subsection (5) above; but

    (b) there is reasonable excuse for his failure to make the disclosure in accordance with paragraph (b) of that subsection.

(8) In the case of a person who was in employment at the relevant time, subsections (5) and (7) above shall have effect in relation to disclosures, and intended disclosures, to the appropriate person in accordance with the procedure established by his employer for the making of such disclosures as they have effect in relation to disclosures, and intended disclosures, to a constable.

(9) A person guilty of an offence under this section is liable—

    (a) on summary conviction, to imprisonment for a term not exceeding six months or a fine not exceeding the statutory maximum or to both; or

    (b) on conviction on indictment, to imprisonment for a term not exceeding fourteen years or a fine or to both.

(10) No constable or other person shall be guilty of an offence under this section in respect of anything done by him in the course of acting in connection with the enforcement, or intended enforcement, of any provision of this Act or of any other enactment relating to criminal conduct or the proceeds of such conduct.".

Concealing or transferring proceeds of criminal conduct

31. The following section shall be inserted in the Criminal Justice Act 1988, after section 93B—

"Concealing or transferring proceeds of criminal conduct

93C.—(1) A person is guilty of an offence if he—

    (a) conceals or disguises any property which is, or in whole or in part directly or indirectly represents, his proceeds of criminal conduct; or

    (b) converts or transfers that property or removes it from the jurisdiction,

for the purpose of avoiding prosecution for an offence to which this Part of this Act applies or the making or enforcement in his case of a confiscation order.

(2) A person is guilty of an offence if, knowing or having reasonable grounds to suspect that any property is, or in whole or in part directly or indirectly represents, another person's proceeds of criminal conduct, he—

    (a) conceals or disguises that property; or

    (b) converts or transfers that property or removes it from the jurisdiction,

for the purpose of assisting any person to avoid prosecution for an offence to which this Part of this Act applies or the making or enforcement in his case of a confiscation order.

    (3) In subsections (1) and (2) above, the references to concealing or disguising any property include references to concealing or disguising its nature, source, location, disposition, movement or ownership or any rights with respect to it.

    (4) A person guilty of an offence under this section is liable—

    (a) on summary conviction, to imprisonment for a term not exceeding six months or a fine not exceeding the statutory maximum or to both; or

    (b) on conviction on indictment, to imprisonment for a term not exceeding fourteen years or a fine or to both.".

Tipping-off

32. The following section shall be inserted in the Criminal Justice Act 1988, after section 93C—

"Tipping-off

93D.—(1) A person is guilty of an offence if—

    (a) he knows or suspects that a constable is acting, or is proposing to act, in connection with an investigation which is being, or is about to be, conducted into money laundering; and

    (b) he discloses to any other person information or any other matter which is likely to prejudice that investigation, or proposed investigation.

    (2) A person is guilty of an offence if—

    (a) he knows or suspects that a disclosure ("the disclosure") has been made to a constable under section 93A or 93B above; and

    (b) he discloses to any other person information or any other matter which is likely to prejudice any investigation which might be conducted following the disclosure.

    (3) A person is guilty of an offence if—

    (a) he knows or suspects that a disclosure of a kind mentioned in section 93A(5) or 93B(8) above ("the disclosure") has been made; and

    (b) he discloses to any person information or any other matter which is likely to prejudice an investigation which might be conducted following the disclosure.

    (4) Nothing in subsections (1) to (3) above makes it an offence for a professional legal adviser to disclose any information or other matter—

    (a) to, or to a representative of, a client of his in connection with the giving by the adviser of legal advice to the client; or

    (b) to any person—

        (i) in contemplation of, or in connection with, legal proceedings; and

        (ii) for the purpose of those proceedings.

    (5) Subsection (4) above does not apply in relation to any information or

other matter which is disclosed with a view to furthering any criminal purpose.

(6) In proceedings against a person for an offence under subsection (1), (2) or (3) above, it is a defence to prove that he did not know or suspect that the disclosure was likely to be prejudicial in the way mentioned in that subsection.

(7) In this section "money laundering" means doing any act which constitutes an offence under section 93A, 93B or 93C above or, in the case of an act done otherwise than in England and Wales or Scotland, would constitute such an offence if done in England and Wales or (as the case may be) Scotland.

(8) For the purposes of subsection (7) above, having possession of any property shall be taken to be doing an act in relation to it.

(9) A person guilty of an offence under this section shall be liable—

    (a) on summary conviction, to imprisonment for a term not exceeding six months or a fine not exceeding the statutory maximum or to both, or

    (b) on conviction on indictment, to imprisonment for a term not exceeding five years or a fine or to both.

(10) No constable or other person shall be guilty of an offence under this section in respect of anything done by him in the course of acting in connection with the enforcement, or intended enforcement, of any provision of this Act or of any other enactment relating to an offence to which this Part of this Act applies".

Application to Scotland of sections 93A to 93D of 1988 Act

33. The following section shall be inserted in the Criminal Justice Act 1988, after section 93D—

"Application of sections 93A to 93D to Scotland

93E. In the application of sections 93A to 93D above to Scotland—
"offence to which this Part of this Act applies" means an offence triable on indictment (whether or not such offence is also triable summarily) other than—

    (a) an offence to which section 1 of the Criminal Justice (Scotland) Act 1987 (confiscation of proceeds of drug trafficking) relates; or

    (b) an offence under Part III of the Prevention of Terrorism (Temporary Provisions) Act 1989; and
"proceeds of criminal conduct" does not include—

    (a) proceeds of drug trafficking ("drug trafficking" having the meaning of the said Act of 1987); or

    (b) terrorist funds within the meaning of section 11 of the said Act of 1989.".

Enforcement of Northern Ireland orders: proceeds of criminal conduct

34.—(1) In section 94 of the Criminal Justice Act 1988 (enforcement of Northern Ireland orders), in subsection (1), for "89" there shall be substituted "88" and the following subsection shall be inserted after subsection (3)—

    "(3A) An Order in Council under this section may, in particular, provide for section 18 of the Civil Jurisdiction and Judgments Act 1982 (enforcement of United Kingdom judgments in other parts of the United Kingdom) not to apply in relation to such orders as may be prescribed by the Order.".

(2) In section 95 of the Act of 1988 (enforcement of Northern Ireland orders in Scotland), the following subsection shall be inserted after subsection (2)—

"(2A) An Order in Council under this section may, in particular, provide for section 18 of the Civil Jurisdiction and Judgments Act 1982 (enforcement of United Kingdom judgments in other parts of the United Kingdom) not to apply in relation to such orders as may be prescribed by the Order.".

Prosecution by order of the Commissioners of Customs and Excise

35. The following section shall be inserted in the Criminal Justice Act 1988, after section 93E—

"Prosecution by order of the Commissioners of Customs and Excise

93F.—(1) Proceedings for an offence to which this section applies ("a specified offence") may be instituted by order of the Commissioners.

(2) Any proceedings for a specified offence which are so instituted shall be commenced in the name of an officer.

(3) In the case of the death, removal, discharge or absence of the officer in whose name any proceedings for a specified offence were commenced, those proceedings may be continued by another officer.

(4) Where the Commissioners investigate, or propose to investigate, any matter with a view to determining—

(a) whether there are grounds for believing that a specified offence has been committed; or

(b) whether a person should be prosected for a specified offence;

that matter shall be treated as an assigned matter within the meaning of the Customs and Excise Management Act 1979.

(5) Nothing in this section shall be taken—

(a) to prevent any person (including any officer) who has power to arrest, detain or prosecute any person for a specified offence from doing so; or

(b) to prevent a court from proceeding to deal with a person brought before it following his arrest by an officer for a specified offence, even though the proceedings have not been instituted by an order made under subsection (1) above.

(6) In this section—

"the Commissioners" means the Commissioners of Customs and Excise;

"officer" means a person commissioned by the Commissioners;

"proceedings", as respects Scotland, means summary proceedings; and

"specified offence" means—

(a) any offence under sections 93A to 93D above;

(b) attempting to commit, conspiracy to commit or incitement to commit any such offence; or

(c) any other offence of a kind prescribed in regulations made by the Secretary of State for the purposes of this section.

(7) The power to make regulations under subsection (6) above shall be exercisable by statutory instrument.

(8) Any such instrument shall be subject to annulment in pursuance of a resolution of either House of Parliament.".

PART VI

SUPPLEMENTARY

Commencement etc.

47.—(1) Sections 42 and 43 shall come into force at the end of the period of two months beginning with the day on which this Act is passed.

(2) Section 48(9) shall come into force on the passing of this Act.

(3) The other provisions of this Act shall come into force on such day as may be appointed by the Secretary of State by an order made by statutory instrument.

(4) Different days may be appointed under subsection (3) for different provisions and different purposes.

(5) Nothing in any provision in Part I applies to any act, omission or other event occurring before the coming into force of that provision.

(6) Where a person is charged with a relevant offence which was committed before the coming into force of a provision of Part II, or (as the case may be) Part III, that provision shall not affect the question whether or not that person is guilty of the offence or the powers of the court in the event of his being convicted of that offence.

(7) In subsection (6) "relevant offence" means an offence in relation to which provision is made by Part II, or Part III, other than an offence created by that Part.

(8) An order under subsection (3) may contain such transitional provisions and savings as the Secretary of State considers appropriate.

Short title, extent etc.

48.—(1) This Act may be cited as the Criminal Justice Act 1993.

(2) The following provisions of this Act extend to the United Kingdom—
Part IV;
sections, 21(1), 21(2) (so far as it amends the first section referred to), 22, 42 to 44, 47 and this section;
Schedules 1 and 2; and
Schedules 3 and 4 (so far as necessary).

(3) Sections 23(2), (3) and (7) to (10), 26 to 29 and 45 extend only to Great Britain.

(4) Sections 17, 19, 20(2), 21(3) and 23(12) to (15) and 30 extend only to Scotland.

(5) Section 44 also extends to the Channel Islands and the Isle of Man.

(6) Otherwise, this Act extends to England and Wales only.

Power of Secretary of State to make grants in relation to combating drug misuse

73.—(1) The Secretary of State may, with the consent of the Treasury, pay such grants, to such persons, as he considers appropriate in connection with measures intended—

(a) to combat or deal with drug trafficking or the misuse of drugs; or

(b) to deal with consequences of the misuse of drugs.

(2) Any such grant may be made subject to such conditions as the Secretary of State may, with the agreement of the Treasury, see fit to impose.

(3) Payments under this section shall be made out of money provided by Parliament.